The Military Fraud and Government Failures of Tim Walz

Josh Manning and Erin Brownback

A POST HILL PRESS BOOK
ISBN: 979-8-89565-051-6
ISBN (eBook): 979-8-89565-052-3

Stolen Valor:
The Military Fraud and Government Failures of Tim Walz

Post Hill Press
New York • Nashville
posthillpress.com

Published in the United States of America
1 2 3 4 5 6 7 8 9 10

For Briley
She loved her family,
Donald Trump,
and most of all Jesus Christ.

and

For my Dad
Who taught me to seek and serve the Lord,
in the ways he did
and beyond.

CONTENTS

PREFACE

There comes a time in every person's life when he or she must choose to speak up about evil or remain silent while the world around them gets dragged down into darkness. This is one of those times. America, a light on a hill for more than two centuries, is cringing under the icy fingers of a creeping shadow. There isn't a thoughtful citizen alive who doesn't feel the chill and see the divide being created between neighbors and friends.

Democracies throughout history start in a state of bondage, and out of that oppression rises great faith. From faith comes acts of courage; from courage comes liberty, and out of liberty comes abundance. Sadly, that's where the cycle peaks and begins its decline. Abundance leads to selfishness, which leads to apathy. Apathy is another word for tolerance, and apathy leads to anarchy, because when everything is tolerated, nothing can be called wrong. Eventually, anarchy leads to dictatorship. For those few democracies that overcome the bondage of dictatorship and return to great faith, the cycle repeats. For others, dictatorship destroys.

For America to survive as a free nation, two things are clear. First, it must be able to manage its abundance. Practices of charity, generosity, and personal sacrifice are at our core. We must press into these to protect us from the lie that it is not our responsibility to take care of our neighbors because we will all be taken care of by the state. And we must put boundaries around the abundance we allow ourselves and our children, so as to prevent selfishness that leads to moral decay.

Second, for a nation to remain free, neighbors must trust each other. In this time of deep political divide, where a news outlet or candidate is incentivized to create distrust, we must look beyond the rhetoric and invite our neighbors into our lives, not because they've earned that right, but because that's the model set before us.

America will never be Heaven on Earth. That joy will come one day for those who know Him. But America can hold the door open for the light that points people in that direction. Or that door can close, leaving the darkness to pull people the other way.

Most democracies that begin to decline do not rise again. But most democracies throughout history do not have something we have. In this modern era of mass communication, the falling action is happening fast. Every time we turn around, we wonder how things have gotten so much worse. But with that speed comes the reality that many Americans are still alive who remember what it means to trust their neighbor and to live contentedly within their means. Many remember what it looks like to be a nation of great faith and courage. And therefore, many are still capable of creating the momentum we need to catapult our country over this chasm of darkness, and onto the solid ground of a bright future.

For everyone, there comes a time when he or she must choose to speak about the evil they see. Even when speaking out may come at a great cost. This is that time.

PART I

Military Fraud

It has been 20 years since dereliction of duty charges played a significant role in a U.S. presidential election. In September 2004, CBS News' "60 Minutes II" aired a report questioning whether President George W. Bush had fulfilled his service commitments to the Texas Air National Guard during the early 1970s. The report quickly fell apart and the ensuing scandal significantly damaged CBS News' credibility, ultimately forcing Dan Rather himself into retirement.

Coincidentally (or maybe not) that same year, John Kerry, the Democratic nominee for the presidency also faced dereliction of duty accusations. A group called the Swift Boat Veterans for Truth challenged Kerry's claims about his own service during Vietnam.

Where CBS News had failed, the Swift Boaters, as they came to be called, succeeded. Their claims that Kerry had lied about his service records and medals took root in the public consciousness and torpedoed Kerry's credibility. Kerry would not recover from the damage the Swift Boaters' testimony inflicted.

After Bush defeated Kerry, the country went 20 years without any serious accusations of military dereliction of duty. Those 20 years ended on August 6, 2024. Not only was military service back on the U.S. political menu, so were dereliction of duty and the National Guard.

Tim Walz, the current governor of Minnesota, a former congressman, and a retired Army National Guardsman beat out Pennsylvania Governor Josh Shapiro for the Democratic vice-presidential spot. To the Harris campaign, Walz came across first like an amiable uncle, and second like someone who wouldn't anger Palestinian/Muslim voters like Shapiro, who is Jewish, would. (The fact that having a Jewish running mate would cost Harris Democrat voters is an issue that falls outside the scope of this book, but every voter should consider what that says about Harris and the Democratic party.)

Walz was instantly visible everywhere. Pictures and videos of him in camo hats showed up in the news.[1] Shots of him in an orange and khaki game vest with his dog and a $1,700 Beretta shotgun[2] circulated on social media.[3] Walz had infamously referred to the conservative red portions of Minnesota as "rocks and cows" territory[4] (which spawned an eponymous and spectacularly anti-Walz Facebook page[5]), but the Harris campaign was clearly making a play for the country's few remaining rocks and cows Democrats.

Walz immediately took to the stage. Where Harris was wooden, insecure, and inarticulate; Walz was animated, overconfident, and could talk a mile a minute without awkward pauses, nervous hand gestures, or cringey cackles. With enthusiasm and a practiced man-of-the-people patter, Walz loudly ordered Donald Trump and his supporters to "mind your own damn business." (That was a bold choice for the man who set up Soviet-style snitch lines for family, friends, and neighbors to report each other for violating Walz's COVID policies.)

All it took was a few minutes listening to learn that Walz, despite his carefully curated avuncular style, was every bit the hardcore leftist that Kamala Harris was. But where she came across as weak and retiring, he came across as hard-nosed and in your face. For all intents and purposes, Walz checked every box when it comes to leftist orthodoxy: Pro-abortion, pro-illegal immigrant, pro-gun control, pro-trans/child mutilation, pro-gay marriage, pro-COVID lockdowns, pro-BLM, pro-tax, pro-spending, pro-marijuana, anti-parental rights, anti-police, and anti-energy.

Corporate journalists sang his praises. MSNBC called Walz a no drama candidate the AP reported Walz was beloved by young voters, the Guardian called him a governor with a history of winning over Republicans, and the Washington Post promptly offered 6 reasons Tim Walz was the right choice.

When it came to citizen journalists, however, things weren't quite as rosy for Walz. Not bound by the establishment media's sycophantic devotion to the Left, citizen journalists on X (formerly Twitter) began digging into every corner of Walz's past. Less than 24 hours after Harris' announcement, accusations of cowardice, stolen valor, and rank embellishment exploded.

Walz spent the nearly 20 years since he retired from the National Guard using his service as a campaign tool, a rhetorical flourish, and an all-purpose key-jangle that can be used to distract from criticism. Because of the way Walz handled his exit from the Guard and the way he has conducted himself since then, serious questions about his integrity have been raised. Specifically, Walz has been accused of cowardice, stolen valor, and rank embellishment. In the process of writing this book, the authors have become convinced beyond a doubt that Walz is guilty. To be clear, neither the authors nor the Guardsmen we spoke with set out to make Tim Walz's military service a political issue. Walz did that by himself.

Divided into two sections, this book ties together the authors' own research, research from citizen journalists, research from national news sources as well as local Minnesota publications, testimony from Minnesotans, and testimony from Guardsmen who knew of Walz or knew him personally. The first section of the book deals with issues related to Walz's military service. The second section deals with Walz's policy positions and the fallout that accompanied their implementation in Minnesota. The vast majority of Walz's positions are extreme and out of line with what average Americans believe, let alone nearly all of us who live out with Walz's spurned rocks and cows.

We, the authors, have reached out to the Harris-Walz campaign, seeking an opportunity to ask Gov. Walz about his military service, the decision he made to leave his unit, how he has represented himself since his retirement, the policies he has advanced throughout his political career, and numerous other details that this book touches on. We also offered him the opportunity to submit comments that we would publish in these pages. As of this writing, neither Walz, nor anyone from his office, nor anyone from the Harris-Walz campaign have responded.

A final note: The public owes a great deal to the citizen journalists who have been excavating Walz's record. In researching this book, we have repeatedly watched articles or evidence we had bookmarked suddenly disappear without explanation. Internet archives would malfunction or tweets with images of official documents would simply vanish into the digital ether. Citizen journalists have done incredible work finding, surfacing, and preserving critical information. This book seeks to do the same, wholistically and in perpetuity.

CHAPTER 1

Cowardice—Sneaking Out

"He snuck out the back door..."

—Lathe Ragels, Command Sergeant Major (Retired)

Of the three charges against Walz—cowardice, stolen valor, and rank embellishment—it makes the most sense to address cowardice first. The other two charges depend to varying degrees on facts that will be established as we consider Walz's alleged cowardice. Cowardice is impossible to objectively prove, but most adults know cowardice when they see it.

We cannot prove that Tim Walz is a coward. But when we examine him and his record, we see cowardice written all over it. There is a chance, however, that it wasn't cowardice that drove Tim Walz to do what he did from late 2004 into 2005. It's possible that what looks exactly like cowardice was actually selfish opportunism. Maybe Tim Walz abandoned his men not because he feared he would be injured or lose his life but because he saw an opportunity for a new life—the DC high life. Maybe he decided it was worth sacrificing the men in his unit for the opportunity to gain power, money, and prestige. Readers will disagree on which is worse—cowardice or selfish opportunism—but one thing is certain: A man whose heart is controlled by either of those nasty traits is not fit to help lead the United States of America.

THE CASE FOR COWARDICE

To establish cowardice, or what appears indistinguishable from cowardice, we have to know why Tim Walz chose to retire before his unit—the unit he was responsible for—deployed to Iraq.

To do that, a timeline of Walz's service is helpful, with particular attention paid to his final enlistment.

Tim Walz first enlisted in the Nebraska Army National Guard in 1981 as a 17-year-old.[6] His last reenlistment was on September 18, 2001—exactly one week after 9/11. Walz claims that he reenlisted for four years,[7] however an NGB Form 22 (the separation and record of service form for Guardsmen leaving the service) for Tim Walz put his end of service date as September 18, 2007, implying Walz actually reenlisted for six years.

Regardless, Walz would eventually retire from the Minnesota Army National Guard in 2005, having served 24 years in total but one or three years less than he reenlisted for in 2001. He served in the 1st Battalion, 125th Field Artillery, a part of the 34th Infantry Division, also known as the "Red Bulls."

Timeline of Walz's Service

- April 1981—Tim Walz enlists in the Nebraska National Guard[8]
- September 18, 2001—Walz reenlists in the National Guard for the last time, for either four years (accord-

ing to Walz) or six years (according to documents provided by Sergeant Major Tom Behrends (Retired))

- August 3, 2002—Walz receives notification of eligibility for retirement from the Guard (20 years of service[9])
- Early 2003—Walz is selected to attend the United States Army Sergeants Major Academy.
- Late summer 2003—First Sergeant Walz deploys with the 1st Battalion, 125th Field Artillery in support of Operation Enduring Freedom (OEF) to Italy
- September 17th, 2004—Walz is conditionally promoted to Sergeant Major (and begins serving as a Command Sergeant Major (CSM) while his packet is submitted to the National Guard Bureau to appoint him to CSM)[10]
- Fall 2004—Notification of Service (NOS) is issued, informing 1st Brigade 34th Infantry Division that it would be alerted to go to Iraq within the next year—Walz's commanding officer Doug Julin meets with leadership of the 1-125th (Walz's battalion) and informs them of NOS[11]
- February 2005—a deployment warning order is issued to the 1-125th Field Artillery Battalion; Walz informs Julin he is running for Congress
- February 10, 2005—Walz files FEC paperwork to run for Minnesota's 1st congressional district[12]
- March 20, 2005—Walz's campaign issues a press release saying he would serve if called, calls him Command Sergeant Major[13]

- March/April 2005—Walz informs Julin in person he is "going forward with the battalion"
- April 1, 2005—Walz is laterally appointed to Command Sergeant Major[14]
- May 16th, 2005—Walz retires from the Minnesota National Guard
- June 2005—Julin meets Tom Behrends at leadership meeting, Behrends informs Julin that Walz has left the Guard and Behrends will be his replacement
- July 14, 2005—The 1-34th Brigade receives deployment alert orders[15]
- September 10, 2005—Walz's record of service is officially modified,[16] resulting in an administrative demotion to Master Sergeant beginning on the day he had previously been promoted to Sergeant Major—September 17th, 2004.
- Fall 2005—The 1-34th Brigade trains for deployment
- March 2006—The 1-34th Brigade, including the 1-125th Field Artillery, deploy to Iraq without Tim Walz

On the issue of cowardice, the first question that must be addressed, both by Walz and his critics, is what drove his decision to retire before the 1-125th deployed. Was it cowardice, political ambition, or some other motivation?

How Walz Framed His Retirement

Walz has claimed variously that he 1) did not know about the upcoming deployment, 2) knew that deployment could be coming,

3) would go if called to deploy, and 4) would work to support his unit by running for Congress if they were deployed.

On March 20, 2005, the Tim Walz for US Congress campaign issued a press release that, among other things, stated the following:

> *Walz... has been previously deployed during his 23 years in the National Guard, including an eight-month deployment during Operation Enduring Freedom.*
>
> *Walz said, "I do not yet know if my artillery unit will be part of this mobilization and I am unable to comment further on specifics of the deployment."*
>
> *Walz is determined to stay in the race. "As Command Sergeant Major I have a responsibility not only to ready my battalion for Iraq, but also to serve if called on. I am dedicated to serving my country to the best of my ability, whether that is in Washington DC or in Iraq."*
>
> *"I don't want to speculate on what shape my campaign will take if I am deployed, but I have no plans to drop out of the race. I am fortunate to have a strong group of enthusiastic supporters and a very dedicated and intelligent wife. Both will be a major part of my campaign, whether I am in Minnesota or Iraq."*
>
> *If called to duty, Walz would leave behind his wife Gwen and four-year-old daughter, Hope.*

That press release marks some of the first of Walz's exceedingly careful wording. Notice the very precise description of his previous deployment, "an eight-month deployment during Operation Enduring Freedom." It is 100% true that Walz was deployed during Operation Enduring Freedom. But it is also true he was nowhere near OEF's active theater. Walz had been deployed to Italy as part of a larger effort to secure US bases overseas during the earlier days of the War on Terror.

Walz's statement that he was "unable to comment further on specifics of the deployment" illustrates the fact a Sergeant Major acting as a CSM (which is what Walz was) has access to advance, confidential information unavailable to the men under their command. This is an important fact that will come up again in the cowardice discussion.

Walz also quickly invoked the rank of Command Sergeant Major and spoke reverently of his "responsibility not only to ready my battalion for Iraq, but also to serve if called on." (He did not mention that he was actually only a Sergeant Major acting as a CSM. He would not be laterally promoted for 12 more days.) He also suggested that his supporters and wife would "be a major part of my campaign, whether I am in Minnesota or Iraq." Clearly Walz and his campaign were acknowledging he could continue his congressional run while deployed.

The press release ends with the somber line, "If called to duty, Walz would leave behind his wife Gwen and four-year-old daughter, Hope."

Harrowing, if not heroic comments, all. This very deliberate wording did three things. First it cast Walz as the hero willing to sacrificially leave his family for his country. Second it made clear Walz would, in fact, leave if called—or at least it stated as much to the voters.

Third, with this wording Walz secured himself a rhetorical escape hatch. "I am dedicated to serving my country to the best of my ability, *whether that is in Washington DC or in Iraq*." In other words, for Walz serving his country could consist either of shooting and being shot at in the Middle East or of snagging a handful of cheesy samosa puffs from a passing hors d'oeuvres tray while schmoozing donors in a swank DC ballroom.

This little linguistic sleight of hand would come to characterize many of Walz's references to his service, retirement, alleged time "in war," and rank. The format is simple and a favorite of the political class: Make a series of positive, crowd-pleasing statements and toss in a throwaway, fine-print sort of line that allows the politician to be technically honest while generally misleading voters.

It's hard to read Walz's press release without getting the *feeling* that he planned to dutifully go if called. After all, that last line incontrovertibly states that if called to duty he would leave his wife and daughter.

Walz's commanding officer, Command Sergeant Major Doug Julin has stated that it was around this time (March or April 2005) that Walz confirmed that he did plan to deploy, despite the fact that he was seeking a House seat.[17]

Walz's March 2005 presser was well designed. If Walz's changed his mind about deploying and just didn't want to go, he could easily point to the functionally fine print in the middle of the release that says "serving my country to the best of my ability, whether that is in Washington DC or in Iraq." And just like that Walz got the benefit of saying that he would serve without actually having to serve.

What Walz Knew and When

Walz's supporters are quick to note that the March press release doesn't prove Walz knew that deployment was coming. PolitiFact tried using (insultingly obvious) rhetorical sleight of hand to defend Walz by way of a "Mostly False" fact check they delivered to J.D. Vance.[18]

Vance had stated, "When Tim Walz was asked by his country to go to Iraq, do you know what he did? He dropped out of the Army and allowed his unit to go without him.... I think it's shameful." PolitiFact purposefully missed the point and responded by stating:

> Walz retired from the Minnesota National Guard in May 2005. He had submitted retirement paperwork five to seven months beforehand, Fox News reported, citing the Minnesota National Guard.
>
> In March 2005, Walz's battalion had been notified about a possible deployment to Iraq within two years, Walz's congressional campaign said in a news release that month, citing the National Guard Public Affairs Office. The Minnesota National Guard said the battalion then received an official order about mobilizing for deployment to Iraq in July 2005, after Walz retired.
>
> Vance's statement misleads by distorting the timeline. Walz had not been "asked by his country to go to Iraq," as Vance said. He had been given a two-year window for a potential, not definite, deployment. And the

> official deployment notice came after Walz's retirement.
>
> Walz has said since before his Army retirement that he left to run for Congress. He filed his candidacy paperwork in February 2005, before the March 2005 notification about the potential deployment.

There are several problems here. First and foremost, nothing that PolitiFact wrote showed Vance's statement to be false. Vance was 100% accurate in stating that Tim Walz's country called and he dropped out. That is exactly what happened, regardless of when Walz filed his campaign paperwork.

PolitiFact also pointed out that Walz filed the paperwork for his congressional run in February 2005, suggesting that proves cowardice couldn't be involved because Walz's battalion wouldn't be notified about possible deployment until the following month.

This, however, rings hollow. Consistently in our interviews with other Minnesota National Guardsmen, we were told that command enlisted (like CSMs) do know about deployments well before the rank-and-file enlisted.

Doug Julin, Walz's commanding officer, said as much to CNN (and put the time of Walz's being informed as fall of 2004).

This advance knowledge is necessarily due to the dual roles that CSMs play in the chain of command and in warmaking more generally. Each CSM is also attached to a commanding officer and functions as the link between that officer and those fighting men. In multiple interviews other CSMs described their role to us as that of parents for the enlisted men—responsible for growing them up, watching after them, conditioning them to complete the mission, and keeping them in line.

That being the case, the CSM absolutely must know well ahead of time that a deployment is coming. Not *if* a deployment is coming but *that* a deployment is coming. And remember, on September 17, 2004, Tim Walz was conditionally promoted to Sergeant Major acting as CSM.

PolitiFact's weakest attempt to counter Vance's accusation was to point out that Walz had filed for retirement five to seven months before actually retiring in May 2005.

Again, nothing there disproves Vance's simple contention that Walz's country called but Walz didn't go. But PolitiFact's cover job raises more questions than it answers. First, if Walz filed for retirement in, say, October 2004, why just two weeks earlier had he accepted a provisional Sergeant Major promotion and acting role of CSM? Just to have a CSM wreath on his insignia? That seems iffy at best given that Walz wouldn't be able to call himself a CSM after retirement unless he simply lied about it (more about that later).

Second, why would Walz commit to the further two years of coursework required after accepting the Sergeant Major promotion if he knew he was going to retire in a few short weeks? To enroll in the United States Army Sergeant Major Academy (USASMA) and get the promotion, Walz would have had to sign, acknowledging the obligations that came with the promotion. In other words, Walz knew what he was agreeing to.

PolitiFact inadvertently put Walz in a binary trap where either option condemned him. On the one hand If Walz planned to retire when he accepted the Sergeant Major promotion, what could the public conclude other than Walz was chasing a rank he knew he couldn't keep for purposes that would almost certainly be less than honorable.

On the other hand if Walz didn't plan to retire when he accepted the Sergeant Major promotion (which seems far more likely), why did he turn and around file retirement paperwork so quickly? The only answer that makes any sense is a very unfortunate one for Walz, Harris, and PolitiFact—Walz knew ahead of time that deployment was coming (as an acting CSM would know), and whether for reasons of cowardice or political expediency, he wanted no part of it.

Another question PolitiFact failed to ask, let alone answer, is if Walz reenlisted on September 18, 2001 for a four-year term (as he claims[19]), why did he seek retirement before his term was up? That retirement, it should be noted, would also come before Walz would be able to complete USASMA school, which reopens that can of worms.

Further complicating that question is Walz NGB 22 which suggests he signed up for six years of service, not four years. That claim would make Walz's choice to proceed with the Sergeant Major promotion make more sense (since he would have enough time to finish training before the end of his hitch), but it also raises all sorts of other unseemly questions about why Walz claimed he only signed up for four years and why he put in for retirement almost three years before his six year reenlistment was over.

Walz's Unsolvable Problem

Tim Walz finds himself in an intractable situation. The timeline makes very clear that he reenlisted with the intention of serving until September 2005 or September 2007. That means he absolutely walked away early. The question is whether he walked away early because of cowardice, to better pursue elected office, or for some other reason Walz never disclosed.

A charitable reading would be that Walz left early so that his run for office would more likely succeed, which would then allow him to better support his unit from Capitol Hill.

But that has its own problems. First, it is certainly possible to run for office while deployed. Tulsi Gabbard did just that in 2019.[20] Second, to actually be of help to his unit, Walz would have to win—a condition that was never assured. And third, it is not at all clear that Walz's presence on Capitol Hill would do more to help the men in his unit than his own presence on the battlefield. (For what it's worth, other Guardsmen have argued that Walz's unit benefited significantly from his absence.)

So far Walz has not clearly indicated why he left his unit or his responsibilities so close to deployment. Without a concrete statement from Walz, many voters will assume cowardice played at least some, if not a very large, role in his choice. And aren't they justified? After all, when was the last time any politician deserved the benefit of the doubt?

If naked political ambition was the driving force behind Walz's decision, he should have the courage to admit that. Leaving your men without their leader so that you can take a shot at one of the cushiest, most entitled, most powerful, most lucrative positions on the planet isn't exactly heroic, but it's not necessarily cowardly either. If he would simply admit he left because a House seat looked better to him than a gunner's seat, Walz could at least put the cowardice discussion to rest. What he would be left with wouldn't be a lot better, but almost anything beats being yellow.

GUARDSMEN RESPOND

While researching Walz's background we spoke with several Guardsmen who knew Walz, had served with Walz, or served adjacent to Walz. Several had very blunt thoughts on Walz's decision to leave before he could be deployed. (We have excerpted and streamlined portions of the interviews to make them more readable.)

Tom Behrends, Command Sergeant Major (Retired)

I got selected [to replace Walz as CSM], and I went to the first staff call we had in June 2005, and Doug Julin just looked at me like, "What the hell are you doing here?" Because I was at the Divarty (Division Artillery) *as a Sergeant Major, and he just looked at me like, "What are you doing here?" And I said, "Walz quit, and I got selected for the position." You could see him turn red like a thermometer—he was pissed because he was the guy's immediate Command Sergeant Major supervisor. I mean...the Colonel was still there as the Battalion Commander, but you don't do that to your Brigade Command Sergeant Major. I mean, if you're going to get out, you tell him. You run it up the ladder. And he didn't say a word.*

Doug Julian is a straight-shooting, rootin'-tootin' CSM, basically, and I think he knew that if he went to Walz... Doug has said to this day "I wouldn't have let him go. I'd have told him, 'You're not going.'"

He lied to Julin over the course of however long they had conversations, when Julin had conversations with his Command Sergeant Majors. "Are you gonna go, or what's your plan," Julin would ask. "Yeah, don't worry, I'm going," Walz would always answer. And then all of a sudden, he's gone.

Actually, you know, if he'd gone to Doug, Doug would have told him, "You can get out, but you're going to be an E6 now and you're getting a less-than-honorable discharge." I think Julin would have hammered him, and I think Walz knew that. So he slid around like a snake and figured out how to get around the system.

And this is being investigated right now—as far as we know nobody knew who the hell he actually went to, because nobody has shown a document that says, "I sign off on Tim Walz getting out as an E9 or an E8, honorable discharge."

The Army actually caught the E9/8 error. We wanted his paperwork out to the state—that's when they reduced him in September 2005. He didn't leave the Army and say, "I didn't finish the school, I need to retire as an E8." The Army had to catch it without his help months later.[21]

I just cannot even believe that a person in that position would quit. Most Command Sergeants Major can't believe it either. It's just absolutely ridiculous. Let me tell you a story. Kyle Miller died on June 29, 2006. He literally had a dream before this mission where he would die. He talked to the chaplain, and the chaplain said, "I can probably get you off this mission if you feel this strongly about it." But Kyle said, "if I don't go on this mission, somebody else dies, gets injured, or takes my place—I will never be able to live with myself." And he went on the mission. They got radar jamming equipment or whatever to put on the Humvees, and on the way back, they backed over a pressure plate, hit a howitzer round, and it blew up, and he died. We've got a bronze likeness of him in our memorial. If you look up Brewster Veterans Memorial on Facebook, we've got a picture of it right there. And we've got this kid, he's kneeling in front of a battle cross with his hand on it. That's Kyle Miller.

I see that memorial and I'm like, "Come to that memorial Tim, sit on one of our black granite benches, and you explain to that kid why it was so damn important that you needed to quit."

We posthumously promoted Miller to E5. He was an E4 when he died, just 19 years old. That's courage. And courage is something Tim Walz didn't have.

My gut feeling, like I said, is if Walz had gone to Iraq, he'd still be hiding under his desk over there to this day. I think he would have been chickenshit. People have told me that if Walz had gone over there, there would have been more body bags than there were.

I really don't know if he quit because he was a coward, or if he realized he was in over his head, or if he didn't want to fight Bush's war. I mean, there are several possibilities, or maybe it's all of the above. I really don't know. He's never said, so how can we know?

Lathe Ragels, Command Sergeant Major (Retired)

Leaders like Walz knew they were going, and they knew damn well where they were going. No arguing about that. Walz was saying "I might have to go" and of course he was playing that to the crowd. And then he went around everybody and slipped out the back door to avoid that damn deployment.

*And my hair is standing up on end just talking about this. Command Sergeants Major lead by example, and when Tim Walz found out that his unit might deploy, his first thought wasn't "I will dig, I will scrape, I will beat down any f****** door to make sure I go." That should have been his drive because that's why he accepted the CSM job he was offered. If that wasn't going to be his focus, he could have just not accepted it. There was no requirement to take it. Nobody forced him into this all-volunteer army, and no one forced him to accept the CSM position. It was offered to him. He could just say, "I don't think I'm ready for that." He could have said that and everything would have been fine. It just befuddles my mind that he would do such a thing.*

Walz knew the deployment was coming. He was privy to information. The command team is privy to all kinds of information. And there were some soldiers in those ranks who might have used that same relief valve Walz used [leaving before deployment] He did it with the information he had, but they couldn't because they didn't know the way he knew.

*Now back in 2003 he sure as hell went to Italy and drank wine and had fun with that damn trip. He took that f****** paid vacation.*

*People defending Walz say he didn't violate anything and his command approved it, but here's the deal: If somebody says I don't want to be the Command Sergeant Major of this deployment to Iraq, as commander I'm telling that guy to get the f*** out of my battalion because I don't want him.*

Just kick him out and move on. It's just easier, especially in the Guard. In the Army, they would not have released him from his contract. Most likely they would have forced him to wander around and change bedpans or they would have deployed him as an E8 somewhere.

In the Army they wouldn't have let him out, but in the Guard... they knew that deployment was going to be ugly, so their idea was let's just cut our losses and move on without this guy.

When you're in the National Guard you accept a paycheck every month. And when you take that check you are agreeing to a commitment. You're going to respond to your nation's call in time of need. And you recommit every time you cash that check. And he did that for 24 years. He recommitted over and over again. It's not just every time you reenlist. It's every time you cash a check. And when the time came, he took the cash but left the commitment.

And of course there's the comparison between Walz and Trump. People talk about his foot issues or whatever and call him a draft dodger, but here's the thing. First of all, thousands of individuals did not get drafted due to medical conditions, but even assuming the absolute worst about him that he made the medical issue up, Trump never made a commitment, right? So I get that there were all kinds of reasons why people avoided the draft, especially with Vietnam—Vietnam was an ugly time and an ugly place—but as far as I'm concerned Gov. Walz is 10 times worse than Trump. He committed to his country and then dodged it. Trump never made a commitment to nothing. Trump never accepted 24 years' worth of checks to do something and then said no, so don't tell me you're better than Trump. You can kiss my rosy red ass.

Tom Schilling, Sergeant First Class (Retired)

I don't have anything personally against Tim Walz. The only thing is his actions—he's done some really serious things that go against what I believe in. I don't really need to speak out, but I always stand up when I know it's the right thing, whether it's easy or not. "It's the right thing to do." I try to live by that phrase. And it's gotten me in trouble in a lot of ways. I ended up deploying to Iraq because of that phrase. I do a lot of stuff I don't want to do, but I always go by, "It's the right thing to do." My wife and I have had over a dozen foster children over the years, and that phrase probably had something to do with that too.

Bailing out if you're a CSM is not the right thing to do. That's not something you really forgive. CSM is a prestigious spot. That's something very few people get. And if you get that spot, a lot of trust goes along with it. And then you turn around and bail? I think that's unforgivable.

And then to go over your commander's head? In the lower ranks if we tried to go past our superior the way Walz did when he wanted out, we'd be reprimanded. Doing an end run like Walz did really isn't an option. You have to go through the chain of command—it's drilled into you. But that's what Walz apparently did.

I think it helps if you think about Tim Walz the way you would think about Tom Brady. Tom Brady trains all year. What's his goal? To win the Super Bowl. So he trains non-stop, and he fixes this and fixes that. He does everything he can possibly do to get to the Super Bowl. Then that Super Bowl Sunday comes and all of a sudden Tom won't leave the locker room. He says, "I don't think I want to go out there because I don't want to get hurt." That's how to think of Walz.

GUARDSMEN'S LETTER

During Walz's gubernatorial race in 2018, retired Command Sergeants Major Tom Behrends and Paul Herr felt so strongly about Walz's abrupt departure from the Guard that they paid out of their own pockets to publish a chronicle of Walz's service from 2003 until his retirement in 2005. The West Central Tribune newspaper in Wilmar, Minnesota published their letter on November 2, 2018.[22]

> *In early 2003 he was selected to attend the United States Army Sergeants Major Academy. The non-resident course consists of two years of correspondence coursework, followed by a two-week resident phase at Fort Bliss, Texas. When a Senior Non-Commissioned Officer accepts enrollment in the course, they accept three stipulations. First, they will serve for two years after graduation from the academy, or promotion to Sergeant Major or Command Sergeant Major, whichever is later. Second, if they fail the course they may be separated from the military. Third, they will complete the course or be reduced to Master Sergeant without board action. Senior Non-Commissioned Officers initial and sign a Statement of Agreement and Certification upon enrollment. The State Command Sergeant Major or Army National Guard Command Sergeant Major counsels the soldier and certifies that the senior Non-Commissioned Officer understands their responsibilities. These stipulations are put in place because the academy is a college level*

school, the military invests a lot of taxpayer money in the student. The military needs to ensure they will get the return on investment that the taxpayers deserve.

In late summer of 2003, First Sergeant Walz deployed with the 1-125th Field Artillery Battalion in support of Operation Enduring Freedom to Italy. The mission was to augment United States Air Force Europe Security Forces doing base security for six months. In no way were the units or Soldiers of the 1-125th Field Artillery Battalion replacing any units or military forces so they could deploy to Iraq or Afghanistan.

After the units return to Minnesota in the spring of 2004, he was selected by high level Command Sergeants Major to serve in the position of the Command Sergeant Major of the 1-125th Field Artillery Battalion.

On August 5th, 2004 he was photographed holding a sign at a protest outside a President Bush campaign rally in southern Minnesota.

On September 17th, 2004 he was conditionally promoted to Command Sergeant Major. The conditions had been outlined to him when he was counseled and he signed the Statement of Agreement and Certification. If the conditions are not met, the promotion is null and void, like it never happened.

In early 2005, a warning order was issued to the 1-125th Field Artillery Battalion, which in-

cluded the position he was serving in, to prepare to be mobilized for active duty for a deployment to Iraq.

On May 16th, 2005 he quit, leaving the 1-125th Field Artillery Battalion and its Soldiers hanging; without its senior Non-Commissioned Officer, as the battalion prepared for war. His excuse to other leaders was that he needed to retire in order to run for congress. Which is false, according to a Department of Defense Directive, he could have run and requested permission from the Secretary of Defense before entering active duty, as many reservists have. If he had retired normally and respectfully, you would think he would have ensured his retirement documents were correctly filled out and signed, and that he would have ensured he was reduced to Master Sergeant for dropping out of the academy. Instead he waited for the paperwork to catch up to him. His official retirement document states, SOLDIER NOT AVAILABLE FOR SIGNATURE.

On September 10th, 2005 conditionally promoted Command Sergeant Major Walz was reduced to Master Sergeant. It took a while for the system to catch up to him as it was uncharted territory, literally no one quits in the position he was in, or drops out of the academy. Except him.

In November of 2005, while the battalion trained for war at Camp Shelby, Mississippi, it received an offer from retired Master Sergeant

Walz. He offered to fund raise for the battalion's bus trip home over Christmas that year.

The 1-125th Field Artillery Battalion was deployed for 22 months in 2006—2007. During this time, they were restricted by Army regulations and could not speak out against a candidate for office. In November 2006 he was elected to the House of Representatives. He claims to be the highest-ranking enlisted service member ever to serve in congress. Even though he was conditionally promoted to Command Sergeant Major less than eight months, quit before his obligations were met, and was reduced to Master Sergeant for retirement. Yes, he served at that rank, but was never qualified at that rank, and will receive retirement benefits at one rank below.

CHAPTER 2

Combat— Turning Your Blood

"If you've been in combat, and you've smelled what it's like and then you witness somebody else claiming to have been there who wasn't, it just turns your blood."

—Tom Schilling, Sergeant First Class (Retired)

Since the nation's founding, military experience has been a definite positive for any presidential ticket. Of America's 46 presidents, 31 served in the military and at least 20 served in combat roles[23]. Many vice presidents served in combat roles as well, including most recently Lyndon B. Johnson and George H.W. Bush, both of whom would later occupy the White House.

Tim Walz served his country in the military and was deployed during wartime once. On this, everyone agrees. Disagreement comes over how Walz has characterized that part of his service. Has he attempted to mislead voters into believing he served in actual combat? An examination of Walz's comments over the years suggests that he used extremely specific wording and targeted omission of relevant facts to create the impression that he served in combat without ever having made an overt claim. Sloppy media reports have supported that impression. Impressions aside, however, the fact of the matter is that Tim Walz never served in combat.

MILITARY SERVICE CLAIMS

We've already discussed Walz's penchant for surgically precise wording. The pattern of precision wording he used to discuss his hasty pre-deployment exit from the Guard shows up again when he, his campaign, or his surrogates discuss his time overseas.

Two days after the Harris campaign announced Walz's addition to the ticket, the *National Review* wrote, "From the beginning of Walz's political career, Walz and his campaign staff have been loose with their characterization of Walz's overseas-deployment record in a way that seems intended to leave the uninformed with the impression that Walz served in a combat zone."[24]

When the *National Review*'s editors wrote "from the beginning," they weren't kidding. In the notorious March 20, 2005 press release, Walz's campaign wrote "He has been previously deployed during his 23 years in the National Guard, including an eight-month deployment *during* Operation Enduring Freedom" (emphasis added).

"During." That's the key word because it can be so easily used to distract if not downright mislead voters. In "Politics and the English Language," George Orwell skewered politicians' tendency to take words and use them to obscure the truth rather than reveal it. He wrote, "Political language... is designed to make lies sound truthful and murder respectable, and to give an appearance of solidity to pure wind."[25]

So, has Tim Walz spent nearly 20 years since early 2005 deliberately trying to take pure hot air and give it the appearance of a solid combat deployment? The answer to that question depends on how much benefit of the doubt you're willing to extend to Tim Walz. Let's look at the facts and then many of the comments Walz has made, comments the media has made, and comments Walz allowed the media to make without bothering to correct them (as far as we've been able to determine).

The Facts

Tim Walz shipped out for a deployment in support of Operation Enduring Freedom on August 3, 2003. He and the rest of the 1st Battalion, 125th Artillery were stationed in Vicenza, Italy to provide additional air base security.

Ahead of the deployment, Tim Walz, then serving as First Sergeant, told the *Mankato Free Press*, "In the big scheme of deployments, this probably isn't too bad. I thought we might end up in Iraq."[26]

Walz served uneventfully in Italy until his unit returned to the U.S. in April 2004.[27]

Anytime Walz, his campaign, or the press talk about Walz deploying in support of Operation Enduring Freedom, what they're referring to is this deployment to Italy to provide additional security to an air base. And they are correct. Walz did deploy in support of OEF. However, not one of them mentions that Vicenza is upwards of 3,000 miles west of Afghanistan. Nor do they ever say that Vicenza is about an hour from the gorgeous Adriatic Sea and just two hours from historic Venice. So when one X user suggested that, like Walz, he too supported OEF "by being a taxpayer," he may have exaggerated somewhat, but perhaps not by much.

These facts considered, Walz was correct when he said in June 2003, "In the big scheme of deployments, this probably isn't too bad."

Walz's 9/11 Remembrance Speech

Inspecting Walz's record more closely, one question we might ask is whether Walz has ever claimed to have been deployed to Iraq or Afghanistan. The answer is no... but only just barely. Normally we don't think of people as "barely" not saying something. They either say the thing, or they don't. In this case, however, Walz barely avoided telling a lie—a lie that was literally written in his own speech.

During the 9/11 Day of Remembrance at the Minnesota State Capital in 2021, Walz spoke not just as governor but also as a veteran. What Walz said during the recorded event did not match his written speech. The relevant portion from the written speech is excerpted directly below:

> In the years after that classroom, I had the privilege of serving in this state's National Guard. I stood one night in the dark of night on the tarmac at Bagram Air Base in Iraq [sic] and watched a military ramp ceremony–a soldier's body being loaded onto a plane to be returned home. And if you've seen it, you don't leave the same. It makes you wonder, what are we doing? What are we trying to get to? And then watching as all of you have been, the confusing last few weeks with the Taliban takeover of Afghanistan.[28]

Walz presumably approved that wording. (If he didn't, that could mean that he blindly goes along with whatever his speechwriter happens to put down.) That wording leaves no space at all between Walz claiming to have served in the Guard and Walz standing on a tarmac at Bagram. Anyone reading that speech would assume that the ramp ceremony occurred during Walz time "serving in this state's national guard." But something significant is missing between the first and second sentences quoted above—several years.

The ramp ceremony Walz referred to took place during a CODEL (Congressional Member Delegation) visit to Bagram (in Afghanistan, not Iraq as the speech inexplicably reads). This ceremony did not occur when Walz was serving in the Guard as his speech so craftily conveys. It took place in 2008, four years after Walz returned from his deployment to Italy and three years after he left the Guard.

Normally this is called lying by omission, but in the context of politics it actually has its own name. According to Harvard researcher Todd Rogers, "paltering" is the act of deceiving someone by telling the truth. Going further, Todd writes, "Rather than misstating facts or failing to provide information, paltering involves actively making truthful statements to create a mistaken impression."[29]

It is true that Walz served in the Minnesota State National Guard. It is also true that he attended a ramp ceremony at Bagram Air Base. It is not true that while serving in the Minnesota State National Guard Tim Walz attended a ramp ceremony at Bagram. Paltering. The American Psychological Association reports "those who palter can do serious harm to their reputations."[30] Truer words.

Added to this paltering is the humiliating fact that a governor's 9/11 remembrance speech placed Bagram Air Base in the wrong country and that that speech is now enshrined for Minnesotans' posterity in the Minnesota Legislative Reference Library.

Now, Walz would certainly defend himself by going to the tape, as it were, and playing back the speech as he gave it, which was worded differently than the written speech.

Speaking from the podium that day, Walz said:

> I had the privilege of serving in this state's national guard and when I left, I had a two-year-old, and when I came home, I had a three-year-old. But as I listened to Jill and I listened to Mariah, the guilt. I came home and my daughter went on, and when you're two and three she knew no difference. That's not true for some. They can't do that. And over the proceeding years of watching us and as our nation changed and as our political systems became more difficult for all of us to understand...
>
> I stood one night in the dark of night on the tarmac at Bagram and watched a military ramp ceremony and if you've seen it which these folks, many have unfortunately, you don't leave the same and it makes you wonder what are we doing, what are we trying to get to and then watching as all of you [indecipherable] of the confusing last few weeks.[31]

Walz's spoken words are certainly less incriminating than his written words, particularly due to the lurching nature of his off the cuff remarks. He flashed from his service, to being home, to the present, back to returning home, back to the present, through some number of years, and finally back to the present. And at that point he picks back up and transitions into the ramp ceremony story, this time simply calling the location "Bagram."

Did punctuating those two sentences the way he did remove the danger of his misleading listeners then and now? Opinions will vary.

The Harris-Walz campaign didn't think so, so for good measure the campaign told Politico's Daniel Lippman that "Walz was referring to a ceremony he attended during a visit to the Bagram Air Base in 2008 while serving in Congress."[32]

The Media's Claims

While Walz has spoken very carefully about his deployment "in support of Operation Enduring Freedom" and has been sure to leave the impression that he might have been in combat or at least in a combat zone, the media hasn't been so careful.

Several different forms of media—local newspapers, national publications, and at least one book—have not just advanced the idea that Walz *could* have been in Iraq or Afghanistan, they have straight out made those claims.

Errors, of course, aren't uncommon in reporting. And as media activism continues to displace journalism, standards sink ever lower. The real question isn't whether incorrect reporting should be corrected. That answer is obvious. The real question is whether a public figure who benefits from incorrect reporting has an obligation to correct that reporting. The answer to that question morally and ethically is also yes. It is not clear, however, whether Walz has ever taken time to correct a single incorrect report of his being in Iraq, Afghanistan, or combat. If he had, why are there so many misleading examples in the public to pull from? Also, why is it so difficult to find cases of Walz correcting the record? Corrections and clarifications on Walz's record have only become widespread since his addition to the presidential ticket.

During Walz's first congressional campaign, the Rochester Post Bulletin reported, "Walz is one of at least 14 servicemen and women from the most recent Iraq and Afghanistan wars to have enlisted for a U.S. House or Senate run this year."[33]

This quote is tricky because it's non-specific. What does "servicemen and women from the most recent Iraq and Afghanistan wars" mean? Does "from" refer to combat, a theater, supporting roles, or general participation in the military during a time of war?

The easiest way to handle this is to excise the extra wording and see what we're left with. If we do that (and clean up the grammar) we get "Walz is a serviceman from war." It's not a stretch to say that the average person would likely read that to mean that Tim Walz saw combat—he was "from war."

As of this writing the Rochester Post Bulletin has issued no correction, clarification, or update for this article.

CBS News reported "Rep. Tim Walz, D-Minn, said that he, along with most Democrats and an increasing number of Republicans, believe sending more troops compounds a bad situation. Walz, a veteran of the war in Afghanistan, said diplomatic and political solutions are needed, not more troops."[34]

This quote isn't anywhere near as challenging as the previous one. "Walz, a veteran of the war in Afghanistan"—that is as definitive as it gets.

As of this writing CBS News has issued no correction, clarification, or update for this article.

Some of the most damning bad reporting came from Joshua Green, not once but twice. The first piece was an early Walz profile from 2006 in *The Atlantic*, where Green served as senior editor. The second sentence of Green's article read "A high school teacher and football coach, he had left to serve overseas in Operation Enduring Freedom."[35]

Whether this is another case of paltering depends on 1) whether you believe Green had an agenda and 2) whether Walz told Green, "I left to serve overseas in OEF," or something similar. One thing is certain—anyone reading that opening paragraph would walk away thinking Tim Walz was *in* Operation Enduring Freedom, not supporting it.

We will return to this article soon because of some other issues, but for now it will suffice to say that as of this writing *The Atlantic* has issued no correction, clarification, or update for this article.

Fast forward 18 years to the day Harris announced Walz as her running mate. Green wrote an article for Bloomberg stating:

> At the time, the Iraq War was ongoing (and going badly), and he stood out as Command Sergeant Major Walz, a 24-year veteran of the Army National Guard, recently returned from serving in Iraq as part of Operation Enduring Freedom.[36]

(Eighteen years have passed, and it appears Green thinks OEF was about Iraq, or he was told that and printed it without checking).

Bloomberg eventually realized Green reported Walz was in Iraq rather than Italy and made the change in a bit of quiet editing. We would report to you when that editing took place, but we have found it impossible to retrieve previous versions of the story. This is uncommon, but not completely unheard of, when dealing with digital publishers. Normally it is possible through different tools (the Internet Archive, Google's cache, Bing's cache, etc.) to access old versions of web pages, including news and commentary articles. In this case, however, old versions simply seem to not exist.

The change was clearly made quickly because Green posted on X the following day (August 7, 2024), taking the blame for the Italy/Iraq mix up. He also posted an image of Bloomberg's correction, which stated: "Corrects [sic] where Walz served overseas in the third paragraph of article published Aug 7."[37] It should be noted that even the correction is incorrect because the original piece was published on August 6.

The Iraq/Italy switcheroo wasn't the only editing Bloomberg did, nor was the incorrect correction the only backstep they took. The original article also included the lines:

> To counter the impression that they were effete, Democrats, with Rahm Emanuel leading the congressional campaign committee, went out and recruited dozens of young veterans of the wars in Iraq and Afghanistan. Walz was one of them.

But a later version of the article nixed the phrase "of the wars in Iraq and Afghanistan" altogether.[38]

Bloomberg acknowledged this edit as well, with another parenthetical correction notice, saying:

> Corrects [sic] to remove reference to wars in Iraq and Afghanistan in fifth paragraph; an earlier version of this story corrected where Walz served overseas in the third paragraph.

So the net sum is that Green originally reported in Bloomberg that Walz served in Iraq and was a veteran of the wars in Iraq and Afghanistan. Then, after several revisions, the article was changed to say that Walz served in Italy and was a young veteran.

As far as we can tell, Walz has never attempted to correct any erroneous reporting of this type. He has, however, publicly and strenuously objected when his record has been questioned.[39] This implies that Walz watches his own media coverage and takes steps to correct incorrect comments that might hurt him politically, but he doesn't appear to do the same for incorrect comments that help him politically.

While it's impossible to know if he ever tried to correct any falsely flattering reports about his military career, it is possible to look at how he has responded to his fellow politicians.

Walz's Comments

In addition to Walz's very carefully worded speeches and statements, dubious claims from the media, and uncorrected comments from fellow politicians, there are Walz's comments about combat and war that came not from careful rehearsing but from unguarded moments.

In 2007 Nancy Pelosi took over as House Speaker. She called a press conference and brought along a number of freshman Democrats, among whom was Tim Walz. By way of introduction, Pelosi thanked Walz for "his service to our country, whether it's in the classroom or on the battlefield."[40]

Walz took to the podium, cracked a joke, and then thanked "my brother in arms, Patrick Murphy." Pelosi had mixed up Walz and then-Congressman Patrick J. Murphy in her introduction, and Walz made the connection between them even stronger.

Walz didn't bother to correct Pelosi's "on the battlefield" description at all. Instead, he doubled down by invoking Murphy as a brother in arms. Murphy actually did serve in Baghdad from

2003 to 2004,[41] roughly the same time when Walz was within striking distance of sunbathers on the Adriatic beaches.

Again, we see the pattern of Walz's careful wording and paltering. Walz and Murphy technically were brothers in arms in that they both served in the military for the same country. But by using that wording, Walz subtly suggested that he and Murphy took up arms together. And by failing to correct Pelosi's praise of his service "on the battlefield," Walz again craftily worded and paltered himself into a position to be lauded as a soldier who fought in combat for his country, when he did not.

Another example, this one much more damning, came by way of Joshua Green's *Atlantic* piece we looked at earlier. After stating Walz served overseas in OEF, Green relayed the story of an angry Walz, incensed that he and two of his students were not allowed into a Bush campaign event in 2004. As the 2004 election approached, Bush came to speak in Minnesota. Walz grabbed a couple of his students, somehow wormed his way onto a campaign bus, and arrived at a quarry where the speech was to take place. Security, however, wouldn't let Walz and his students pass, despite their having their tickets and IDs. Walz later recalled the incident, saying, "As a soldier, I told them I had a right to see my commander-in-chief." It's not clear exactly why Walz thought being in the military gave him the right to see the president, but that's neither here nor there.

Then, for a reason Green didn't report, Walz began to suspect he might be arrested. So he looked at the Bush staffers barring his way and asked if they "really wanted to arrest a Command Sergeant Major who had just returned from fighting the war on terrorism." So to get his way, Walz trotted out the idea of combat service ("fighting the war on terrorism"). It's hard to imagine a more cowardly and entitled response to not being admitted to a political rally.

Green's article has been available online since 2006. As of this writing no correction has been issued. As far as we can tell, Green still believes Walz told Bush staffers that he had just gotten back from actually fighting the war on terror. Neither have we been able to find any example of Walz correcting this report. That does not mean that he hasn't, but it does mean that if he has corrected it, he hasn't done so effectively. Obviously *The Atlantic* would quickly issue this sort of correction at Walz's prompting. We can only conclude, then, that Walz has not contacted the magazine because 1) he didn't/doesn't know about the story, 2) he wanted Green and the Bush staffers to believe the egregious lie that he was in combat, or 3) he is fine with *The Atlantic* making it sound like he was in combat because it benefits him. None of those options are good for Walz. The idea that he didn't know about the story is unlikely. And the ideas that he either actively misled or refused to correct the record for political gain (or worse as a cheap get-out-of-jail-free card) are outrageous.

If the *Atlantic* piece shows what an angry Walz said to get his way, a video that the Harris campaign posted (and later very much came to regret) demonstrates what a relaxed Walz would say when he found himself with a non-critical, friendly audience.

On August 6, 2024, Harris announced Walz as her running mate and @KamalaHQ posted a video[42] to X showing Walz speaking at a small gathering in 2018. The crowd was very friendly and applauded as Walz recited boilerplate Democrat anti-Second Amendment talking points. The applause may have over-excited Walz because after it died down, he made a shocking comment:

> I've been voting for common sense legislation that protects the Second Amendment, but we can do background checks. We can do CDC

> research, we can make sure we don't have reciprocal carry among states, and we can make sure those weapons of war, *that I carried in war*, is [sic] the only place where those weapons are allowed.

"That I carried in war." The fact that no one in the Harris campaign caught this before it went out is remarkable. Well, it's remarkable if people in the Harris campaign knew Walz had never been to war. But it's also possible that those in the Harris campaign were under the impression Walz had been in war, which might just be the strongest argument demonstrating Walz's stolen valor. Walz has stolen it so completely that his own campaign believes the lie that he was in war. Or worse, the campaign knows that's a lie but believes they can spread it anyway because the public won't know any better.

If Walz's myriad of dubious military claims had been raising the temperature, this was the claim that sent the crock pot (or just crock?) lid into orbit. There was no surgical wording here. No squishy syntax. No "well, it could mean this or that." This was it. Walz put it down big, plain, and straight—I carried weapons of war in war.

There's actually more than one problem here. The war claim is big by itself. But there's also the ludicrous suggestion that Americans can walk into any old shop or stop by a gun show and walk out with a "weapon of war" like he carried "in war." That's not true, and it reveals that Walz is either pitifully uninformed (doubtful) or doubly deceptive (far more likely).

Whether deployed to Afghanistan, Iraq, or Italy, Walz would have been issued an M-16A2 rifle or an M4 carbine. Those rifles have fully automatic, 3-round burst, and single shot select fire trigger systems. That means that with the flip of the safety lever, the shooter can choose how the weapon will fire. M16s and M4s are considered Class III weapons under the National Firearms Act. Anyone who wants to own a class III weapon must submit detailed information to the Bureau of Alcohol, Tobacco, Firearms and Explosives (ATF), along with their fingerprints, a letter of approval from their local chief law enforcement officer, and a $200 fee. The turnaround for approval can be up to 90 days. Those are weapons of war, and they are not easy to get ahold of in the US.

The civilian weapon that Democrats most love to refer to as a "weapon of war" is the AR-15 sporting rifle. The AR-15 looks nearly identical to the M16 and M4. The key difference is that the AR-15 does not offer select fire options. There's no automatic or 3-round burst option. AR-15s will only fire once for each pull of the trigger. That is the same way that ranch rifles and semi-automatic shotguns have worked for generations. Those are civilian weapons that do *not* belong on the battlefield.

So what do we make of Walz's "weapons of war" claim? Does he think that the streets are flooded with M4s? Doubtful. If that were an issue, we would hear about it anytime one showed up at a crime scene. (Unless the crime scene was in a blue city where Democrat politicians allow the wholesale slaughter of young minority men and women. The establishment media doesn't publicize those crimes.)

If Walz is trying to make his audience believe that the streets are flooded with M4s when he knows that's not true, he can only be called a liar.

And what if he thinks that AR-15s are actually weapons of war? Does he think that we've been outfitting platoons with civilian sporting rifles and sending them overseas to fight terrorists? We can only hope he doesn't.

As is the continual theme with Walz, neither option is a good one. If he's saying that our streets are overflowing with M4s, then he's a liar. If he's saying that AR-15s are all over American bases in the Middle East, he's an absolute idiot.

The core issue here, of course, is the "I carried in war" part. There is absolutely no way to interpret this other than "I, Tim Walz, carried a weapon of war in war." There was no "*in support of*" qualifier, no "*for* the war in Afghanistan" obfuscation, no "*during* Operation Enduring Freedom" sleight of hand. No, this was straight up "I, Tim Walz, carried a weapon of war in war."

As soon as the video spread, the blowback was strong and swift. The campaign tried to ride it out, but on day four they broke down. Lauren Hitt, a Harris campaign spokeswoman issued a statement saying:

> In making the case for why weapons of war should never be on our streets or in our classrooms, the governor misspoke. He did handle weapons of war and believes strongly that only military members trained to carry those deadly weapons should have access to them, unlike Donald Trump and JD Vance who prioritize the gun lobby over our children.[43]

But here we have more sleight of hand. Hitt doesn't tell how Walz misspoke. She just says that he misspoke, and then she repeats the misleading talking points Walz spouted in the video.

Political finagling like this is exactly why voters often feel the governing class are essentially a group of overgrown children. The Harris-Walz campaign's statement is the equivalent of a child saying "I'm sorry" when the child just wants to get out of trouble and has every intention of doing the exact same thing again as soon as you turn your back.

That behavior is excusable in children because it can be trained out. It is inexcusable in the political class precisely because it can't be trained out. Walz finally crystallized everything that he had been implying, suggesting, and paltering and that the media had been offering him. He took credit for being *in* war when he really wasn't. And it was a lie.

We asked Walz about the issues above, but he declined to respond.

GUARDSMEN RESPOND

We spoke with several Guardsmen about Walz's claims relating to combat. Several spoke up. (We have excerpted and streamlined portions of the interviews to make them more readable.)

Don Baker, Sergeant First Class (Retired)

This pisses me off. I didn't hear that "in war" quote before they announced Walz was going to be in the VP spot. Then I heard him say it in the video, and I about fell out of my chair. My wife had to calm me down because I knew it was a BS statement right off the bat.

I've got brothers and sisters who are veterans who have never been to combat. And they would never falsely make that claim. There's no way.

No one will ever convince me that Walz just misspoke. He was trying to embellish something that wasn't there.

By the way, no veteran speaks that way: "A weapon of war like I carried in war." No veteran would make that mistake.

I was in Iraq. We were extended while we were there. We were in war. Tim was not. And he should have never made that statement. They pulled the pin on that grenade and got caught, so then they had to throw themselves on it.

That whole "weapon of war" rhetoric is right out of the liberal left playbook because if anybody has half a brain, they would know that nobody carries an AR-15 in combat and nobody carries an M4 on the streets.

Tom Schilling, Sergeant First Class (Retired)

When we were in combat, we were in a situation where we didn't know if we were coming back because mortars... they don't really care where they fall. If your number's up, your number's up. Anybody that's been in combat and has been to a military funeral in country while deployed for someone who was walking right next to you a little bit before and is now dead—that's an experience that you won't forget. What I'm saying is if you've been in combat, and you've smelled what it's like, and then you witness somebody else claiming to have been there who wasn't, it just turns your blood.

Tim Walz owes an apology to the American people for what he did. He has dishonored the American people and all the people who are serving as well. The difference between the Army and the Guard is we do our training and then go live back among the people. When he dishonors us, we have to live with what he's done everywhere we go in the community.

If I saw him and we sat down, I'd say, "You owe the American people an apology. What you did is disgraceful, and you need to come clean. Not that it's going to fix everything, but you owe it to the people to say, 'I made a mistake.'"

Tom Behrends, Command Sergeant Major (Retired)

He's lying about weapons of war and lying about what's on the streets, and then he says, "I carried it in wars." He's got three lies in that video clip right there, and we're supposed to trust him to be second in command in the United States? You can't make this stuff up.

CHAPTER 3

Fraudulent Rank—Living the Lie

"He lived the lie so damn long that now he just believes the lie himself."

—Tom Behrends, Command Sergeant Major (Retired) on Walz's decades long rank fraud

The third dubious military claim Walz has repeatedly made is that he retired from the National Guard as a Command Sergeant Major. No honest critic questions whether or not Walz held the rank of CSM. He did. The core question is whether Walz has been honest in the way he has presented his rank to the American people. And the answer to that question is a resounding no.

An inspection of the claims Walz has made, the claims he has allowed others to make, and the relevant documents yielded damning results. But the worst came from the United States military itself. Tim Walz has spent nearly 20 years deceiving the people of Minnesota. And since Kamala Harris catapulted him to the fore of national politics, Walz's is now trying to deceive the entire country.

Understanding how Walz's deception works requires understanding how he became a CSM and how he would ultimately end up losing that rank.

HOW WALZ BECAME A CSM

In 2003, Tim Walz was selected to attend the United States Army Sergeants Major Academy (USASMA)

On September 17, 2004, he received a promotion to the rank of Sergeant Major and began serving as acting CSM.

His service as CSM was conditional. For the rank to become permanent, Walz would need to complete a special program through the USASMA. CSMs Behrends and Herr described it well:

> The non-resident course consists of two years of correspondence coursework, followed by a two-week resident phase at Fort Bliss, Texas. When a Senior Non-Commissioned Officer accepts enrollment in the course, they accept three stipulations. First, they will serve for two years after graduation from the academy, or promotion to Sergeant Major or Command Sergeant Major, whichever is later. Second, if they fail the course they may be separated from the military. Third, they will complete the course or be reduced to Master Sergeant without board action. Senior Non-Commissioned Officers initial and sign a Statement of Agreement and Certification upon enrollment. The State Command Sergeant

> Major or Army National Guard Command Sergeant Major counsels the soldier and certifies that the senior Non-Commissioned Officer understands their responsibilities. These stipulations are put in place because the academy is a college level school, the military invests a lot of taxpayer money in the student. The military needs to ensure they will get the return on investment that the taxpayers deserve.

On April 1, 2005, Walz was laterally appointed to Command Sergeant Major.[44] Walz would later claim (and allow others to claim) that he retired holding that rank. The truth, however, is more complicated and highly damaging to his record and reputation.

CLAIMS

For nearly 20 years (2005-2024), Walz repeatedly described himself as a retired Command Sergeant Major. Colleagues, event hosts, and the media described him similarly.

Claims Walz Made

On March 20, 2005, six months after Walz began acting as CSM and 11 days before he was laterally appointed to CSM, his congressional campaign issued a press release that included the line "Tim Walz currently holds the rank of Command Sergeant Major in the 1-125th Battalion." After retiring, Walz built part of his political identity on claims that he was a "retired Command Sergeant Major" or he "retired as a Command Sergeant Major." For two decades he called himself the highest-ranking noncommissioned officer to ever serve in the House. Walz branded himself as *the* retired CSM.

The X account @NoVA_Campaigns[45] has compiled multiple supercut videos of Walz calling himself a retired CSM. Examples include:

> "I'm a retired Command Sergeant Major…"
>
> Referring to someone else introducing him: "This is Congressman Tim Walz; he's a retired Command Sergeant Major in the Army artillery."
>
> "I'm a schoolteacher, a retired Sergeant Major…"
>
> "As a 24-year veteran of the Army National Guard and a retired Command Sergeant Major…"
>
> "As a retired Sergeant Major in the Army National Guard out of Minnesota…"
>
> "I retired out as Command Sergeant Major…"
>
> "I spent 24 years in the military, congressman, as a Command Sergeant Major…"
>
> "I am a retired Command Sergeant Major in the Minnesota National Guard."
>
> "I am a retired Sergeant Major in the Army National Guard."
>
> "… what I consider to be the responsibility and the privilege of being the highest-ranking enlisted personnel ever to serve in Congress—Command Sergeant Major."

> Referring to someone else introducing him: "He said you have a visitor that's coming. This is Congressman Walz from Minnesota. He's a retired Sergeant Major in the Army."
>
> "I have a unique privilege in Congress. By being elected from this district and being a retired Command Sergeant Major, I am the highest-ranking enlisted soldier to ever serve in Congress."
>
> "I'm Congressman Tim Walz. It's a real honor to be able to pay tribute to the 34th Red Bull Infantry Division and to your families and friends as you prepare to deploy in support of Operation Iraqi Freedom. As a 24-year veteran of the National Guard and the Red Bull Division, and a retired Command Sergeant Major..."
>
> "Shortly after I was elected, I got the opportunity to go out to Walter Reed Army Medical Center [sic] and visit some of our wounded warriors. And there was this young man there coming back from Iraq, recovering from his injuries. And they said, 'This is Congressman Walz, he's a retired Sergeant Major in the Army.'"

Claims Walz Allowed Others to Make

Over that same nearly 20-year span, Walz has allowed others to introduce him as a retired CSM. In the clips we reviewed not once did he correct any speaker. In fact, he often nodded in agreement. Here are some examples.

Interviewer speaking: "When you first came to Washington, you were a retired Command Sergeant Major in the Army National Guard… [Walz nods in agreement]"

Introduction at event: "He served 24 years including in Operation Enduring Freedom, retired as a Command Sergeant Major which makes him the highest-ranking enlisted soldier to ever serve in the United States Congress."

Introduction on the House floor by OEF veteran Rep. Patrick Murphy: "Madam Speaker, I yield 30 seconds to the gentlemen from Minnesota, the highest-ranking enlisted soldier to ever serve in the United States Congress, Command Sergeant Major Tim Walz."

Walz responds: "Thank you, Madam Chair. I thank the gentleman."

Campaign commercial: "Tim Walz is one of those everyday people, coach to the state champs, teacher of the year, Command Sergeant Major…"

Introduction at event: "Congressman Tim Walz—a member of the Armed Services Committee and Veterans Affairs. Democrat of Minnesota. Highest ranking enlisted soldier ever to serve in Congress. Enlisted in the Army National Guard at 17. Retired 24 years later as Command Sergeant Major and served with his battalion in Operation Enduring Freedom."

Introduction at event: "With service in both the Nebraska National Guard and then the Minnesota National Guard, he retired as a Command Sergeant Major."

Speaker described Walz: "[He is a] congressman and retired Army Command Sergeant Major with time in combat..."

Introduction at event: "...the Command Sergeant Major Gov. Tim Walz of Minnesota—state champion football coach and now our joyful warrior, please welcome Gov. Tim Walz of Minnesota."

Introduction at event: "He's a coach to the state football champs, and he's a Command Sergeant Major in the Army National Guard."

Introduction at event: "I'd like to introduce you to my favorite coworker who achieved the rank of Command Sergeant Major in the Army National Guard and someone who proudly wears the Red Bull whenever he can. So please join me in welcoming our governor, a veteran, Tim Walz."

Introduction at event: "A retired Command Sergeant Major in the National Guard, he represents Minnesota's first congressional district and is the ranking member of the House Veterans Affairs Committee. A member of American Legion Post 11 in Mankato Minnesota, he was the creator and sponsor of the American Legion

> Coin Bill and was a valuable ally in the passage of numerous other veteran-centric pieces of legislation. Please give a warm American Legion family welcome to Rep. Tim Walz."
>
> Kamala Harris: "To his fellow veterans, he is Sergeant Major Walz…"

The day Harris announced Walz as her running mate, her campaign website launched a page about Walz. The sixth paragraph of that page described Walz as "The son of an Army veteran and a retired Command Sergeant Major in the Army National Guard himself."[46] Two days later, however, that wording (and the rank's capitalization) would be replaced with "The son of an Army veteran who served as a command sergeant major…"[47]While it's easy to edit a website to get a candidate out of hot water (as long as people don't know how to find old versions of the site), Walz created a completely un-editable problem when he was in the House. Years earlier Walz became enamored with "challenge coins" and began collecting them. These metal, coin-sized tokens are common in the military community (and have spread to the political community as well) and can serve as a sort of calling card, reward, or keepsake. He began minting his own "Tim Walz" challenge coins while in Congress.[48]

The problem for Walz is that the series he minted in the House featured the Command Sergeant Major rank insignia, which is distinguished from other Sergeant insignia by a star circumscribed by a wreath.[49] It's unclear how many of the CSM coins are floating around in the open, but MPR News reported Walz ordered 500 coins at $4 each a few months after he took the governor's office in 2019. Those coins did not feature the CSM insignia.

Based on all of these examples, it's clear that from at least March 20, 2005, (the campaign presser issued six months after his conditional CSM promotion) until the Harris-Walz campaign website was updated on August 8, 2024, Tim Walz wrote, said, affirmed, and even struck into coinage the claim that he was a retired Command Sergeant Major. The only question remaining was about his retirement. Could he legitimately call himself a retired Command Sergeant Major?

Walz's Rank at Retirement

On his NGB Form 22 (the paperwork Guardsmen fill out as part of their separation from the Army), Walz listed himself as CSM/E9 with a date of rank (when he became a CSM) of April 1, 2005 (11 days after his campaign claimed his rank was Command Sergeant Major). To a casual observer that seems reasonable. After all, it wasn't like Walz had been drummed out of USAMSA. He simply retired before completing all the required work. But as reasonable as that might seem to the casual observer, the U.S. military is anything but casual.

On September 10, 2005, just shy of four months after Walz retired, a correction to his NGB 22 was filed. The correction read:

> THE ORIGINAL REPORT OF SEPARATION AND RECORD OF SERVICE (NGB 22) FOR THE ABOVE NAMED INDIVIDUAL IS CORRECTED AS INDICATED BELOW.
>
> 5a. READS AS: "CSM"
>
> CHANGED TO READ: "MSG" [Master Sergeant]
>
> 5b. READS AS: "E9"

CHANGED TO READ: "E8"

6. READS AS: "05 04 01" [April 1, 2005]

CHANGED TO READ: "04 09 17" [September 17, 2004]

In other words, on September 10, 2005 the Army National Guard administratively demoted Tim Walz from CSM/E9 to MSG/E8, retroactively back to September 17, 2004. And while this action was definitely a demotion, it's important to be clear that an administrative demotion is just that—administrative. As much as Walz's many critics would like, this demotion was not punitive.[50]

Walz was demoted because he failed to meet conditions one and three of the Army Sergeants Major Academy. Students who enroll in the program agree that they will serve for two years after graduating or being promoted to Sergeant Major or Command Sergeant Major, *whichever is later* (condition one). And they agree that *if they do not complete the course*, they will be reduced to the rank of Master Sergeant (condition three).

At the time of his retirement, Walz had not completed the USASMA requirements, which is why he was demoted to Master Sergeant. The NGB 22 correction form mentioned above did just that—it made Walz's administrative demotion official and gave him the rank of Master Sergeant, retroactively effective as of September 2004.

This is where things get tricky. Walz takes great pride in saying he retired as a Command Sergeant Major. And without knowledge of the timeline, program requirements, and paperwork, non-experts find it hard to attack any of Walz's claims. After all, on the day he walked away from the Guard, his NGB 22 said he was a Command Sergeant Major.

It took four months for the slowly grinding wheels of government bureaucracy to realize what Walz had done. He had left the Guard before his demotion could catch up with him. In other words, he had gotten out of the Guard with the rank of CSM because of essentially a paperwork delay/mistake.

Walz knew the conditions of his provisional CSM rank. He knew that if he didn't hold up his end of the deal, he would lose the rank and be demoted. He had agreed to those conditions when he started USAMSA. But it appears that instead of working with the personnel division to clean things up before he retired, Walz retired and went on his merry way. We have asked Walz to produce any paperwork or witnesses that would show otherwise, but the request has gone unanswered.

If the abstract idea of rank makes it difficult to understand why so many people are angry at Walz, consider the same case, only involving a medal instead of a rank. Imagine that, thanks to a paperwork error, Tim Walz had been given a Purple Heart that he didn't deserve. Walz would know he hadn't earned the Purple Heart, and the Guard would know that as well… once the paperwork got cleared up. But government paperwork is slow, and that would give Walz an opportunity to retire before the paperwork would catch up to him. So he could leave the Guard, taking with him a Purple Heart he didn't deserve.

That illustration alone should make plain that Walz is in the wrong, but let's make it absolutely crystal clear. Imagine four months have gone by since Walz retired, and the paperwork has finally caught up to him. The military revokes his Purple Heart, but for the next 19 years Timothy J. Walz continues boasting that he retired with a Purple Heart. It's on his campaign website. People introduce him as a National Guardsman who retired with a Purple Heart, and he nods in agreement. He introduces himself as a Guardsman who retired with a Purple Heart. He says it during speeches. He even has a personal challenge coin made that features a Purple Heart on one side. To describe that behavior as contemptible would be a wild understatement. And that is exactly how Walz has behaved for the last 19 years—contemptibly.

Walz's defenders might object to the characterization above, saying that a Purple Heart is a bad example because of its inherent sacredness. That's fine. We could cede that point, but it hardly makes a difference. Replace "Purple Heart" above with "Bronze Star" (perhaps a bad example since those can only be earned in combat). The medal doesn't matter because the principle's the same. Claiming something you didn't earn but temporarily possessed because of slow paperwork is repulsive. Doing so to garner votes from a trusting public is vomitatious. There is simply no defense.

THE TRUTH

The day after Harris announced Walz, the Minnesota National Guard spoke out. Army Lt. Col. Kristen Augé told Just the News that while Walz had conditionally held the title of Command Sergeant Major, he "retired as a master sergeant in 2005 for benefit purposes because he did not complete additional coursework at the U.S. Army Sergeants Major Academy."[51]

Army Col. Ryan Cochran would bring the entire sorry tale to a definitive close when he emailed reporters on August 13th, 2024. In his capacity as Director of Manpower & Personnel for the Minnesota National Guard, Cochran, said:

> Governor Tim Walz... was promoted to sergeant major (E-9) on September 17, 2004, and immediately began serving as the command sergeant major for the 1st Battalion, 125th Field

> Artillery while his packet was submitted to the National Guard Bureau to appoint him to command sergeant major (E-9). Once approved by NGB, he was laterally appointed to command sergeant major (E-9) on April 1, 2005. He retired from the Minnesota National Guard on May 16, 2005. Our records do not indicate when he made his request to retire. Leadership reviews and approves all requests to retire. *He was administratively reduced to master sergeant (E-8) on May 15, 2005*, because he did not complete all required U.S. Army Sergeants Major Academy coursework.[52]

"He was administratively reduced to master sergeant (E-8) on May 15, 2005." That is as clear a statement as possible. On May 14, 2005, Walz was a Command Sergeant Major. On May 15, he was administratively demoted to Master Sergeant. On May 16, Walz retired from the Minnesota National Guard.

Just 45 days after having been laterally appointed Command Sergeant Major, Timothy J. Walz—the man who claimed for 19 years to be a "retired Command Sergeant Major" retired as a Master Sergeant.

GUARDSMEN RESPOND

Tom Behrends, Command Sergeant Major (Retired)

I got back here from Iraq, back to the First District of Minnesota, where he was the representative. People were calling him a retired Command Sergeant Major all the time, and I was like, "He's not that. "I mean, he didn't finish the school, he didn't do his two years afterward.

*While in Iraq I met a CSM from Iowa. I later learned that he and four other high-ranking soldiers were traveling together by helicopter to their base in Assad. Well, some sons of b****** had been lying out in a field for over two weeks. They'd been waiting for a helicopter to fly over, and finally one did. They shot it down, then finished it off with an RPG, and it killed everyone on board—all of them. They're all buried at Arlington, in a mass tomb, basically a grave. And I'm just like, "These Command Sergeants Major out there shed blood and led their people into battle, and they don't have a voice anymore. The ones who died there... someone's got to bring out what Tim Walz has done."*

*My Colonel told me, "I wish I had never met him, because then we wouldn't have to expose Walz as a liar." That's the sad part about it. There's nothing wrong at all with being a Master Sergeant. The crazy thing I found out today—this son of a b**** actually made a challenge coin with the House of Representatives on it and the Command Sergeant Major rank in the corner. It's just like, "For Pete's sake, man." I think he lived the lie so damn long that now he just believes the lie himself.*

Lots of other Guardsmen are ready to come forward. They want this guy to be court-martialed at this point. They want him reinstated into the Guard, court-martialed, and then discharged with whatever the hell discharge he actually deserves, which is not honorable.

And I honestly think it is a possibility that that could happen. When you look into what he did for political gain, more or less profiting off lying about his rank... I thought about that before too. He kind of slipped through the cracks on the Hatch Act, not being on active duty. But back in '04, if I remember correctly, he was called a political activist by an editor at the Star Tribune. They said that's what he was back then. He held up a sign that said, "Operation Enduring Freedom Veterans for Kerry," and he was still in the Guard at that point. I've got a copy of that, and here's this jackass standing there in shorts campaigning for a politician. That's a Hatch Act violation for sure.

So he's lied about his rank, profited off of those lies, and violated the Hatch Act. If that's not worth considering him for a court-martial, what would be?

Lathe Ragels, Command Sergeant Major (Retired)

*Listen, if he wasn't a sergeant major this wouldn't be such a big deal to me because people embellish their service all the damn time. It's just stupid, and it's incompetent punks just doing stupid s***, but if he wasn't purporting to be a Sergeant Major, it wouldn't be such a big deal to me. Him leaving his soldiers in the lurch when he was deploying and him making false claims that he didn't know that deployment was coming—b*******, flat b*******.*

Now if he had gone—if he hadn't snuck out the back door—they could have made do with him as CSM. But the unit would have been far less effective than they were with Behrends because from all reports Behrends was a consummate CSM. He was what a CSM is supposed to be. That's what reports from his soldiers and from his leaders were. Everybody agreed.

If Walz had gone as CSM, I think he would have basically been doing whatever he could to avoid anything hard and done whatever the commander said without question and not had the hard conversations that, although rare and private, are expected between the commander and the CSM. That's the kind of CSM he would have made—in other words, a completely worthless one. He wouldn't have been effective. I knew he never was a leader. He didn't understand it. He didn't know how to protect the troops in the right way. He didn't know how to demand their professionalism. He just wasn't it.

Don Baker, Sergeant First Class (Retired)

Yeah, I hate to admit it, but I do know Tim personally. But that's why I'm bewildered. He has presented himself in this political platform and now he is misleading people as to who he really is. He's a snake... a wolf in sheep's clothing. I don't know how else to describe it. He has entered the political world. I don't know if I want to use the word "pandered," but he at least "catered" to a group of people that will keep him in power. That put him in the power and keeps him in the power.

Command Sergeant Major school is two years. And then the Guard Bureau requires after they get done with their schooling to be in that position for two years. So that's the obligation that was presented to Walz, and he willingly said "yeah, I'll do that."

*Then all of a sudden, we get an alert order, a warning order, and he goes all "f***, I don't want to go to Iraq. So now I guess I might just as well retire".*

And hell no he didn't retire as a CSM. He didn't fulfill the obligation he signed up for, and now he's constantly saying he retired as the highest NCO rank that was available, which is a bunch BS. He retired as a Master Sergeant, E8.

I think about the conversations I've had with mutual friends, other people that I've been in the Guard with. They all talk about the same thing I talk about, how disappointed we are in him. And that's what I would like everybody to know.

I know there's some Guard members that loved him. They absolutely adore him. They think he's the best thing since sliced bread. And I ask them why, and the answer I get is "oh, Tim's a good guy." I'll ask them what he's done for them, ask them to talk nuts and bolts. Why do you adore him? They just say, "he's a nice guy, he's a good guy." It's like the opposite of what happens when you ask people who don't like Trump why they can't stand him.

"He's mean." It's the same thing. It doesn't have anything to do with politics—it's just feelings. But none of these Guardsmen who adore him can tell you why, other than that he's just a nice guy. What kind of a CSM would that be? He may have made a good CSM, however we will never know. Tim hasn't shown me good leadership, his no action after the George Floyd riots that resulted in the destruction of several city blocks being burned to the ground. His response when questioned about it referring to not getting trained soldiers, "what did the mayor want a bunch of nineteen year old cooks" and of course not caring about rural Minnesota his reference to "the land of rocks and cows." He inherited a budget surplus spent it all and probably put Minnesota into a deficit.

PART II

Government Failures

Part I of this book demonstrated the ways Tim Walz has stolen valor in an effort to advance his own career and standing. He has stolen it by claiming a rank that was not rightfully his, when other servicemen worked for that rank and retired with it honestly. He has stolen valor by claiming to have been in combat when he was not, and saying that in the face of others who risked and lost their lives on behalf of our nation. And he has stolen valor by abandoning his men when he knew they were being called up to serve in war.

Just as John Kerry's presidential attempt was torpedoed by the honesty of the Swift Boat Veterans, so too would the exposure of these lies alone be enough to turn the tide against Walz. But the truth is, his stolen valor is only the beginning.

Walz's dishonesty continued beyond his military fraud. On Sept. 23, 1995, he was arrested for driving drunk at more than 40 MPH over the speed limit. Nebraska State Trooper Stephen Rasgorshek took him to jail for driving 96 MPH and failing a field sobriety test, breath test, and a blood alcohol test [53] After his arrest and conviction, he resigned from his position of coaching 9th grade football, and the following year moved to Minnesota to escape the embarrassment.[54] He took a job at Mankato West High School where he taught history, but his criminal record prevented Walz from being hired as a football coach. Instead, the school allowed him to serve as an unpaid assistant on the football team.[55] In spite of the minimal role he played as a volunteer, Walz would later make claims that he had led this high school football team to a state championship.

In 2006, Walz ran for Congress, and his DUI resurfaced. Instead of owning it, like he said he would when he pleaded guilty, his campaign manager lied for him and said he was driving fast because he was afraid of the State Trooper following him, and he was not intoxicated. She said he failed the sobriety tests because of ear damage suffered during his continued service with an artillery unit, and his spokesperson told the media that it was because the trooper refused to speak up."[56] Like the National Guardsmen he served with, Trooper Rasgorshek has also since spoken out against Walz's deceptions, and the court transcripts have demonstrated that these were lies.[57]

By the time Walz ran for governor and 2018, and especially during his second campaign in 2022, the mantra had developed in the public, "Tim Walz Lies."[58]

So much of Walz's story is built on lies, and yet somehow, he was still able to get elected to office. In his time in Congress, and to a far greater extent as governor, he has pushed a radical agenda that does not match the midwestern values of most Minnesotans.

Despite being handed an $18 billion surplus, he introduced the largest budget in state history and took it into the red, raising taxes another $10 billion while slapping schools with over 65 unfunded mandates.[59] He has implemented DEI requirements in schools and created a governmental DEI task force that suppresses free speech and dictates how businesses need to run. And in even more radical ways, he has passed legislation that has transformed the climate of his state.

Walz has long concerned himself with children's sexuality, going back to his days as a schoolteacher. His interest in directing children's attention to sexual matters has only gotten worse over time. In office, Walz has worked aggressively to expose children to sexually explicit content in school libraries that would once have been confined to adult bookstores. He has also pushed to provide chemical castration drugs and body mutilating and sterilizing surgeries for children, while keeping parents in the dark.

As if the mutilation of children's bodies wasn't enough, he has pushed in every way possible for the dismantling of babies' bodies, both inside the womb and out. His brutal abortion positions are a megaphone for his identity politics, and include being in favor of the truly gruesome practice of partial birth abortion, and discarding living babies that survive abortion attempts. Walz has also promoted policies that make it easy for girls even younger than 10 to have abortions with no questions asked. His actions have created in Minnesota a haven for child sex traffickers.

While Walz is adamant that medical decisions of gender mutilation and abortion should be personal and available to anyone, even our youngest citizens, his mandated health decisions and authoritarian COVID lockdowns exposed him as an aspiring dictator with a decidedly Marxist bent. Like many politicians, Walz used "emergency powers" to sideline his state's lawmakers and rule through executive fiat. But for Walz, dictatorial power was too good to let go. His 130 executive orders included a Soviet KGB-style snitch line for neighbors to report on each other, and he sent people door-to-door giving vaccine shots. After endless emergency extensions and 15 months of calling the shots, Walz's own legislature had to step in and revoke his powers.

While Walz did anything but allow people to make their own healthcare decisions when it came to COVID, he all but publicly encouraged complete lawlessness during the race riots of George Floyd and Black Lives Matter. As the Twin Cities erupted in violence, theft and arson, Walz delayed long enough to let more than 1,000 buildings burn before calling in the National Guard, and only then did it under pressure. He undermined the police, sacrificing them on the altar of critical race theory, and cared more about the rights of criminal arsonists than law enforcement officers or law-abiding citizens.

To understand these actions and policies that seem straight out of a dystopian novel, one must understand Walz's deep attachment to China, and the influence it has had on him throughout his military and government career. It explains why he's traveled to the communist country more than 30 times and met with its senior leaders. While his Marxist ideologies might come wrapped up in a jovial, midwestern package, their roots spread deep through the soil beneath the surface. Walz's communist sympathies may be one of the greatest accomplishments of the Chinese Communist Party in modern times.

Knowing all of this about him, it is a wonder that he was ever elected, and even more so that he was reelected, especially after he let his cities burn. But beyond that, American citizens were truly shocked when he was chosen to be the running mate to strengthen the Kamala Harris ticket. Her campaign, however, seems more drawn by the impact Walz's ideologies can have on the nation, than they fear the damage they could do. Part II exposes why.

Due to the speed of mass communication in this modern era, and because of the need to capture content before it disappears from online, this book has been put together with rapidity prior to the 2024 presidential election. The following chapters are not exhaustive examinations; they are an exploration of how perverse and damaging Walz's beliefs are. Reading them will provide more than enough information to see what he would certainly do on a national level.

The following pages can be read as research, but they should also be seen as a stark warning of the path our country will take if Harris and Walz win in November.

CHAPTER 4

Sexualization of Children—He Celebrates It

"Governor Walz didn't just rubber-stamp pro-LGBTQ legislation, he held celebrations."

—Kat Rohn, Executive Director of OutFront Minnesota[60]

Tim Walz left the National Guard and his deployment overseas to run for Congress. As a U.S. Representative for Minnesota's 1st Congressional District under the Democratic-Farmer-Labor Party, he served a more conservative constituency. But even at that time his liberal sexual leanings began to show. Then as governor, his true colors came out.

A CHAMPION OF SEXUAL CONFUSION

In Congress, Walz championed an agenda of sexual liberty for adults. He advocated for alternate sexual lifestyles by working to repeal "Don't Ask, Don't Tell," and he was also an early supporter of same-sex marriage. [61] As governor, he turned his attention to the sexual behaviors of children.

Promoting Homosexuality

In 1999, Walz, then a 35-year-old social studies teacher at Mankato West High School, took it upon himself to create and advise the school's first Gay-Straight Alliance (GSA) club. His goal was to introduce and normalize gender and sexual topics among young students. From this early time, Walz's commitment to encouraging children to explore deviant sexual practices is evident. His actions as an educator pushed a social agenda at the expense of the academic and emotional well-being of the students.

In 2023, in the Walz for Governor pride parade, Walz walked alongside children who were brought out to march for gay rights. These children, used as symbols in a broader political debate, were paraded along with men wearing S&M harnesses and dog masks, drag queens, and the Dykes on Bikes motorcycle gang. Instead of showing concern for their exposure to such perversion, Walz praised the children who participated, referring to them as the "real stars" of the parade.[62]

"Conversion Therapy"

If a minor does end up expressing an attraction to a person of the same sex or some other unconventional attraction, particularly after being introduced to sexual ideas of this nature since he or she was in kindergarten, Walz has taken significant steps to prevent any adult from legally counseling that child in a direction other than toward that attraction. Even if a child expresses that he or she has an unwanted sexual attraction, counselors may not use what Walz calls "conversion therapy" to work through with that child any trauma, abuse, or neglect. Even if those issues could be the root of sexual confusion, counseling is off limits if it is given with the intention of changing the child's unwanted attraction. Counselors stand in jeopardy of losing their licensure if they do so.

Walz has taken control of the psychological and counseling arena in two ways. In July 2021, he signed Executive Order 21-25 which prohibits state agencies from allowing medical assistance or state funding to be used to counsel minors in any direction except toward a same-sex or alternate attraction. In addition to cutting off state resources, Walz has also supported local ordinances that ban counseling minors away from these attractions.[63] These combined efforts make it extremely difficult, if not impossible, for licensed professionals to legally offer therapy to minors in Minnesota other than to encourage same-sex and alternate attractions.

Tampon Tim

In a move that doubled down on normalizing gender confusion among children, Walz mandated that menstrual products, including tampons, be provided in boys bathrooms in Minnesota public schools. The mandate was part of Walz education finance bill. Endorsement of the legislation helped ensure that it became law which he signed in 2023.

The policy does not allow schools to opt out of providing female products in boys bathrooms. In fact, tampons must be present in all Minnesota schools' boys' bathrooms as early as grade four. Because many elementary schools share bathrooms among grades, this means that small boys may have tampons in their bathrooms from the time they're in kindergarten. This policy pushes an agenda that ignores biological realities and confuses young minds at a critical stage of their development, encouraging boys to see tampons as a normal part of their bathroom experience.

Laws like this are not about practicality or supporting children's well-being; they are about enforcing a radical ideology. The law is clear and must be complied with, meaning that even if a school district sees the absurdity [64]of putting tampons in boys' bathrooms, they are legally obligated to do so. This is not just a waste of resources—it's an active endorsement of a belief system that encourages children to question their biological sex. Instead of supporting children through the confusion of adolescence and helping them be comfortable in their own bodies, Walz's policy pushes them further down a path that could lead to chemical and surgical mutilation of their bodies that have irreversible consequences.

CHEMICAL ALTERATION AND SURGICAL MUTILATION OF CHILDREN

In a time when countries commonly thought of as progressive, like Great Britain, Sweden, Finland and others, are reevaluating their approach to gender transitions for children and restricting or banning medical interventions related to gender dysphoria, Walz is moving full steam ahead. Because minors are regretting their decisions, even to the point of suicide, and treatments are posing serious health risks such as impacts on bone density and fertility, and due to a recognition that many children presenting with gender dysphoria also have co-existing mental health issues that require comprehensive assessment and support, many transgender clinics are closing, and many parents have brought lawsuits against them.

Walz, on the other hand, has set a stage in Minnesota for children to be groomed into what leftist activists call alternative sexual lifestyles. Not only has he encouraged same-sex attraction to the point of making it illegal to counsel against it, but his actions have gone further into promoting gender confusion for kids, who may embrace gender dysphoria when they find that "being gay" isn't special enough. To this end, Walz has created policies to lure children down a path of chemical and surgical alteration.

Executive Order on "Gender-Affirming Care"

In March 2023, Walz signed an executive order that bans any restrictions on what is euphemistically called "gender-affirming care" in Minnesota, which includes chemical and surgical "gender treatments" for minors.[65] This order instructs state agencies to ignore out-of-state subpoenas and requests for extradition for children who come from other states to seek gender altering treatments. This means that Minnesota will not cooperate with legal actions or investigations from other states that have laws restricting or banning such procedures, and in turn, Walz's laws create a legal shield for kids seeking these treatments and people providing treatments to kids in Minnesota.

By banning cooperation with other states' legal frameworks, Walz's executive order undermines parental rights, allowing minors to undergo irreversible procedures without their parents' knowledge or consent, potentially leading to tragic outcomes such as regret, psychological harm, and long-term health consequences. This order could also turn Minnesota into a haven for traffickers of minors who have a financial or personal interest in physically changing a child's sexual appearance.

When Walz created this executive order, he emphasized the need for "immediate protection," and framed the order as a necessary and urgent action to safeguard children's rights to change their gender, particularly in the context of increasing restrictions in other states. Curiously though, the following month he signed the "Trans Refuge" bill that accomplished the same thing, leaving people to wonder about the need for immediate protection, and if he believed there were children lined up for chemical and surgical alterations who could not wait for several weeks until his new law was signed.

"Trans Refuge" Bill

Following his executive order, Walz signed the "Trans Refuge" bill in April 2023, further cementing Minnesota's role as a sanctuary state for minors seeking gender alterations.[66] While the executive order could be rescinded by a future governor or challenged legally, the "Trans Refuge" bill codified the instructions outlined in the executive order into state law creating a more permanent and legally enforceable framework.

This legislation explicitly states that Minnesota will not cooperate with out-of-state investigations or subpoenas involving minors who travel to Minnesota for gender altering procedures, This statement violates the Full Faith and Credit Clause of the U.S. Constitution which requires states to respect the "public acts, records, and judicial proceedings of every other state." Refusing to cooperate with out-of-state subpoenas and court orders when it comes to the transing of children positions Minnesota as partially seceding from the Union.

But more significantly than that, the bill states that a person "acting as a parent" or pretending to be a parent can give permission for these procedures. This phrase allows someone other than a child's legal parent or guardian to authorize significant medical interventions, such as hormone treatments and mastectomies, vaginoplasty, and phalloplasty. That could include someone who has their own agenda in wanting the child's sexual appearance to be changed, or someone who doesn't have any legal responsibility for the child. In addition, the bill allows Minnesota courts to take "temporary emergency jurisdiction" in custody cases where children come to Minnesota for chemical and surgical alterations that are illegal in their home state. This means that the state of Minnesota can take children away from parents living in other states.

Walz's radical stance and legislative agenda prioritize identity politics over the safety and well-being of children. By making Minnesota a sanctuary for these shocking and often disfiguring procedures, Walz is sending a message that Minnesota will actively protect those who seek to bypass the laws and protections in their home states. His actions give adults a far greater ability to traffic kids across state lines and exploit vulnerable children who don't even live in his state. He not only pushes for and protects policies that allow this, he celebrates them.

CELEBRATIONS

"Governor Walz didn't just rubber-stamp pro-LGBTQ legislation, he held celebrations and celebratory signings," said Kat Rohn, the Executive Director of OutFront Minnesota, the state's largest LGBTQ+ advocacy organization.[67] For Rohn, a biological woman who identifies as non-binary, this is something to be praised; for others, it is cringe-inducing.

Walz has marked one piece of legislation after another by events and public celebrations. When he signed his euphemistically named "gender-affirming care" executive order, he held hands with a 12-year-old boy going by Hildie Edwards who has tried to appear as a girl, and who testified in support of the bill. The signing of the Trans Refuge Bill was accompanied by a significant event, where Walz was joined by LGBTQ+ activists and families with transgender children. The event took place at the Minnesota State Capitol and was attended by various LGBTQ+ advocates, including Representative Leigh Finke, the first openly transgender lawmaker in Minnesota and the bill's author. At another celebration for Walz's ban on what he calls "conversion therapy" for minors, the event was again marked by public displays of support from gender and sexual confusion activists, with the governor positioning Minnesota as a leader in LGBTQ+ rights.

But celebrating the availability of these drastic medical interventions for children is deeply troubling, particularly given the irreversible nature of many of these procedures. Such public celebrations are not only tone-deaf, but exploitative, particularly when children are used as political symbols to push an agenda that is harmful. Using a 12-year-old child as a symbol of these controversial policies at a high-profile, politicized event turns a complex personal problem into a public spectacle that prioritizes ideology over the well-being of the child. These actions, combined with the sweeping nature of the policies themselves, paint a picture of a governor who is more interested in advancing a sexual agenda than in safeguarding the rights and safety of all children in his state.

PEDOPHILIA

In the wake of the push for same-sex attraction and gender confusion, another sexual agenda is on the rise. The normalizing of pedophilia has been advancing for a decade. In 2013, the American Psychological Association declassified pedophilia as a disorder, and reclassified it as an orientation, using the same arguments they used for homosexuality—some people are born attracted to children, they are unlikely to change their attraction to children, etc. Since then, efforts have been made in media and entertainment to blur the lines on what is sexually acceptable between adults and minors. In keeping with this trend, and Tim Walz's other sexual agendas for children, Minnesota has now become a place where pedophilia is protected.

In February 2023, transgender lawmaker Representative Leigh Finke, a biological male who has been open about his chemical and surgical alterations to present as a woman, shepherded the Take Pride Act through the legislature. The Take Pride Act updated the existing Minnesota Human Rights Act in three significant ways. The Act added "gender identity" as a protected class in the state. According to the updated language, "gender identity" was defined as "a person's inherent sense of being a man, woman, both, or neither." This change extended legal protections against discrimination based on gender identity.

The Act also repealed protections for landlords who were renting out rooms in their homes or a portion of the place where they lived. The update forbade the owner from choosing a roommate or tenant based on their gender or gender identity. The repeal of this protection could put a young female homeowner, for instance, in harm's way by forcing her into a potentially unsafe situation of living with a biological male who is much bigger and stronger than she is. In its effort to advance a personal agenda, it imposed a one-size-fits-all approach. It does not actually take care of citizens, and it also assumes that the enforcers of this law can know what factors make someone accept a roommate or not.

The most egregious, however, of the changes brought by the Take Pride Act was the removal of language that read, "'Sexual orientation' does not include a physical or sexual attachment to children by an adult." This clause ensured that pedophilia could not be legally protected under the guise of sexual orientation. When it became apparent that this language had been removed, Representative Harry Niska introduced an amendment in the Minnesota House that passed with unanimous bipartisan support (126-0) to maintain the language that clarified pedophilia was not protected under "sexual orientation." However, when the act came back from the Conference Committee where the language between the House and the Senate is reconciled, the language on pedophilia was gone again. A push was made to remove the protections against pedophilia, and this time a vote of 68–62 along party lines removed the protections for children.

What happened can only be understood in the context of Tim Walz's approach to governance. Walz decided he was going to govern in a 100% party- centric way. He was not going to work with Republican legislators or look for middle ground; instead he was going to govern with an iron fist of Democratic Party ideals. In the state senate at this time, Democrats had a one vote lead, 34–33. And the understanding among the legislators was that Senator Erin May Quade, a member of the Queer Caucus, said that the Democrats weren't going to be able to govern if they didn't take this language out, because her one vote on all other issues would determine if they had a majority or not. Quade was willing to hold the state's entire legislative session hostage. This is the level of extremism that Tim Walz is overseeing in his party, and this prompted the second vote that passed along party lines. Walz then signed the bill that removed these protections for children.

So to be clear, if a second-grade teacher in Minnesota talks about being attracted to children, he cannot be fired from his job. If he is fired, he can sue the school district. This could result in him receiving a large amount of taxpayer dollars in a settlement and/or being reinstated to work with those children.

The removal of this protective language is a reckless move that prioritizes the protection of pedophiles and the advancement of identity politics over the safety and well-being of vulnerable children. Governor Walz, by signing this bill into law, aligned himself with the most radical left-wing actors in the nation. He prioritized his personal and political agenda over protecting minors from exploitation despite warnings and protests from those who saw the inevitable consequences that occur each time steps like this are taken. His decision has awakened his constituents and the nation to the fact that he has made Minnesota a safe haven for people who would seek to exploit children.

WRAP UP

Tim Walz has stuck his stake in the ground on advocating for the sexualization of children. From insisting on their exposure to explicitly sexual content at a young age, to prohibiting counseling toward anything but alternate sexual desires, to championing the gender mutilation and chemical castration of kids, he has made known his commitment to identity politics at all costs. He has opened the doors for adults to play a role in this sexualization in many ways, and as is always the case when minors are exploited, girls end up pregnant. So when Tim Walz talks about freedom and "minding your own damn business," what he is really saying is, "Leave us alone while we sexualize and trans your children and abort babies."

CHAPTER 5

Abortion—Settle Down

"Nancy Pelosi [told] me to 'settle down' after I was particularly enthusiastic about the pro-choice stance we were taking. 'Let's focus on making sure our policies get implemented effectively rather than just broadcasting our commitment to them.'"

—Tim Walz

Nearly one million abortions are reported per year[68] in America. Of the women who undergo those abortions, 73.8%[69] of them say they felt pressured in some way to have an abortion according to the *Journal of American Physicians and Surgeons*. Abortion is one of the most hotly contested issues in the United States since the issue of slavery. One side holds fast to the desire for sexual liberty and what they call "reproductive justice." The other champions the idea that every human deserves life, and women, children, healthcare workers and taxpayers deserve to be protected from the potential dangers and trauma caused by abortion. Tim Walz is on the former side.

Long positioning himself as a staunch advocate for abortion, Walz's legislative career, from his time in Congress to his tenure as governor, is marked by expanding the abortion industry and removing every safeguard possible that once stood between a woman and the choice of ending the life of the child inside her womb.

Walz's colleague Nancy Pelosi, one of the most prominent advocates on the side of abortion, once remarked that Walz was so extremely pro-choice that he needed to "settle down." Walz laughed about this comment, repeating it at his 2018 gubernatorial campaign events. While Walz's name has become synonymous with the promotion of abortion, some see this as a sign of progress. For others, his legacy is a painful reminder of a system that is sacrificing children for pleasure, and leaving women to grapple with the consequences of decisions made under pressure and in moments of vulnerability. Walz's legacy on abortion plays out in five main ways.

PROTECTING WOMEN

During the 50 years of Roe v. Wade's rule in America, allowing abortion for any reason up until the moment of birth and even following birth, individual states created many protections to prevent women from being pressured into an abortion, being harmed by an abortion, or having an abortion they would regret. These safeguards included requiring abortion facilities to have safe medical standards, women be allowed to see their ultrasounds if they so desire, abortions performed on minors be reported to parents or the police, and standards that would be routine in any medical procedure. In every situation in which Tim Walz was given an opportunity to vote on such protections for the women of the nation, or ensure the safety of women in his own state, he chose to remove these safeguards and instead encourage the business of abortion at all cost.

Child Interstate Abortion Notification Act (H.R. 748)—2015

Minors are easy targets for predatory adults who may have a vested interest in ensuring that a pregnancy is terminated without the knowledge of the minor's parents. In some cases, these adults may be responsible for the pregnancy, creating a conflict of interest where the adult coerces the minor into an abortion to avoid legal consequences. For these reasons, this bill was created to safeguard young women from coercion by adults who want to conceal an unwanted pregnancy, particularly if that pregnancy involves criminal or abusive behavior. The Child Interstate Abortion Notification Act makes it a federal crime to transport a minor across state lines to obtain an abortion, thereby circumventing parental notification or consent laws in the minor's home state.

While the protection of minors is a central part of many American laws, particularly the trafficking of minors across state lines for the purpose of sexual exploitation or coercive crime, Tim Walz as congressman voted against this protection for young women. His voted in the House to allow adults to take children across state lines to secretly get abortions without parental consent.[70] And as governor, he solidified this opportunity for everyone in his state, including predatory adults, by repealing Minnesota's parental notification requirement. This is perhaps the most contentious of Walz's actions. For many parents, this safeguard was a crucial part of protecting their children, ensuring that they were involved in what is undoubtedly one of the most significant decisions a minor could make, and being able to provide the follow-up care and support necessary for medical or emotional issues that occur in the aftermath of an abortion.

Walz's decision to remove this requirement is a direct assault on the role of parents in guiding their children through difficult times. It reveals a desire to make decisions for children at a state level, rather than respecting the role and rights of parents, or simply put, to replace parents with the state.

Repeal of Abortion Restrictions—2023

Instead of supporting or implementing protections for women and minor girls from the dangers of abortion, as governor, Walz repealed the safeguards Minnesota had in place. When he repealed the parental notification requirement, he made sure that the people who worked at abortion facilities were the only ones who knew a girl was making this decision. And abortion facility generates roughly 50% of its generated income from abortion, so it stands to gain financially from an abortion being done on a minor, and is therefore significantly biased in guiding her choice.

Walz also repealed the requirement that abortion facilities gain an informed consent from patients. This means he removed the requirement that they provide state-mandated information about the procedure before an abortion, including the medical risks associated with abortion and pregnancy, as well as alternatives to abortion, such as adoption. The standard process for all medical procedures is that a patient is informed of the potential risks, and consents to the procedure. But Walz deemed that an unnecessary part of preparing a woman for an abortion in Minnesota, and a hurdle for an abortion facility to make a sale.

In addition, Walz repealed the 24-hour waiting period that a woman is given to process this information prior to a procedure. This would be similar to a patient showing up at a hospital, saying she wanted back surgery, putting on a gown and going into the operating room. She would never have been informed of the risks, legally consented to the procedure, or reviewed the process with a doctor or anyone else in her life. Walz repealed all of these protections for Minnesotan women in 2023 so as to make Minnesota a more abortion friendly state.

Protect Reproductive Options (PRO) Act—2023

In addition to removing these safeguards that protect women, Walz signed into law the PRO Act on January 31, 2023 following the overturn of Roe v. Wade. This act functions similarly to a state-level Roe v. Wade. It makes having an abortion a fundamental right under Minnesota state law, and creates a legal rampart against any protections for women, children, medical workers or taxpayers. The Act allows for abortion for any reason and at any time. While neighboring states created regulations on abortion following the federal Supreme Court's ruling on Roe, many people have called Walz's Protect Reproductive Options (PRO) Act a "dangerous" and "extreme" direction for abortion. "Make no mistake," said David Hann, the Minnesota Chairman of the Republican Party, "this extreme bill provides for taxpayer-funded abortion, on-demand, up until and even after birth."[71] With this legislation, Walz removed reasonable and necessary protections, endangering the health and safety of preborn children, women and minors.

PROTECTING CHILDREN

The abortion debate in the United States is often framed around the issue of women's rights and bodily autonomy, but just as there are two patients involved with any pre-natal procedure or operation, there are two lives to consider in every abortion. Over the years, prenatal babies have been protected by both federal and state regulations, particularly in the later stages of pregnancy. These safeguards are based on the belief that unborn children deserve certain rights, including protection from pain and from particularly gruesome procedures like partial-birth abortions.

However, during his time in Congress and as governor, Tim Walz staunchly opposed legislation that restricted late-term abortions, partial-birth abortions, or abortions based on discriminatory factors like sex or race. Walz's commitment to abortion rights often comes at the cost of necessary protections for unborn children, leaving them vulnerable to practices that are widely regarded as extreme, and that many find morally abhorrent.

Partial-Birth Abortion Ban Act (H.R. 3660)

Walz's political record supports the gruesome practice of partial birth abortion, which has been banned in America because of its graphic violence against children. A partial-birth abortion is a procedure enacted during the second or third trimester that involves partially delivering a baby feet-first, typically until only the head remains inside the womb. At that point, the physician uses scissors to puncture the base of the fetal skull while the head is still in the birth canal. Once punctured, the contents of the skull are suctioned out with a vacuum, which causes the skull to collapse. After the skull has been collapsed, the child is fully removed from its mother's body.

The Partial-Birth Abortion Ban Act aimed to eliminate this grisly procedure, which was highly controversial due to its gruesome nature, and which is now banned in the U.S. Walz, however, voted to continue allowing partial birth abortion on pre-natal babies, as is consistent with his entire voting record.[72]

Born-Alive Abortion Survivors Protection Act (H.R. 4712)

Sometimes an abortion fails, meaning an infant is born alive after a procedure is used to end his or her life prematurely. For instance, in a saline abortion, salt water is injected into the womb and creates a toxic environment, burning the delicate fetal tissue and causing severe dehydration and internal organ damage, which typically leads to death. However, 15 to 20% of premature babies typically survive induced-labor abortions to be born alive.[73] These infants can live without any care for as long as several hours after birth, but are left to die. A nurse who brought this to the public's attention witnessed one of them being taken to a utility closet and left there to die, while her hospital maintained that staffers left the babies in "comfort rooms" until they expired. Either way, they were being left to die without any attempt at medical care.

The Born-Alive Abortion Survivors Protection Act was created to protect these infants from neglect, or any further harmful action following being born alive. Walz voted against this protection for newborn infants that requires healthcare practitioners to provide the same level of care to an infant born alive after an attempted abortion has failed, as they would to any other newborn. His vote was to allow an infant to be left to die in a "comfort room" or a utility closed. In opposition to Walz's gruesome stance, this bill ultimately passed in the House by a vote of 241-183.

Prenatal Nondiscrimination Act (PRENDA) (H.R. 3541)

Tim Walz vocally opposes gender and race discrimination, but he doesn't vote to protect females or racial minorities when they are in the womb. In 2011,[74] "The Global War Against Baby Girls[75] presented troubling evidence that male infants were being born throughout the world in far greater quantities than throughout history due to mass female feticide. Large-scale female feticide has been taking place in the U.S. for years, particularly among certain sub-populations. Walz's vote on the Prenatal Nondiscrimination Act was to allow the termination of baby girls because they are girls.

Similarly, this bill also bans abortions performed on the basis of a prejudice against the race of the child. Like a sex-selective abortion typically happens on baby girls, a race-selective abortion typically occurs when the father is a different ethnicity than the child's mother. For instance, if a White woman is pregnant by a Black man, or an Asian woman is pregnant by a Hispanic man, this mixed-race baby might be aborted simply because of this ethnic diversity. Ending the life of a child because it is racially not preferable is horrifying, but not to Walz who voted to allow this practice to continue.

Walz claims to be a champion for gender and racial equity in many of his political positions. But even as experts have demonstrated that these selective abortions are on the rise in the United States, he opposes gender and racial protections for pre-natal children, claiming that it is too difficult for an abortion facility to determine why a woman is having an abortion. This stance though flies in the face of the fact that he facilitated the passage of the Matthew Shepard and James Byrd Jr. Hate Crimes Prevention Act in Congress.[76] This measure expands the 1969 United States federal hate-crime law to include crimes motivated by a victim's actual or perceived gender, sexual orientation, gender identity, or disability, in addition to their race, color or religion. So while Walz believes he can know the motivation for someone committing a crime, he doesn't believe he can know the motivation for someone having an abortion.

Pain-Capable Unborn Child Protection Act (H.R. 1797 & H.R. 36)

Only six nations in the world allow abortion on demand for any reason up to the moment of birth. Among those six are countries guilty of placing religious minorities in concentration camps, starving their own people, imprisoning political opponents, and offering people with disabilities an option for assisted suicide but not for care—and the United States[77]. China is also one of these countries, and perhaps because of Walz's great admiration for China, or perhaps because of his great admiration for abortion, he has voted at each opportunity to allow abortion past the point where pre-natal children have been determined to feel pain.

The Pain-Capable Unborn Child Protection Act, and other similar acts were created to ban abortions after 20 weeks of pregnancy, based on the evidence that a pre-natal child feels pain at this stage. This bill includes exceptions for cases where the pregnancy endangers the life of the mother, which accounts for less than 1% of abortions, and for abortions that are the result of rape (including rape by incest), which accounts for 1% or less of abortions.[78] While many want to protect unborn children from "gruesome late-term abortions," and even with these exceptions, Tim Walz still voted against all versions of this protection for pre-natal children.

On all these votes and others, including the Sanctity of Human Life Act (H.R. 23) that declares that human life begins at conception and that the Constitution protects the rights of the unborn, Tim Walz voted against any protections for fetal life.[79] For Walz, abortion rights are a political battleground, a place to assert his progressive prowess. But for others, his extreme positions that dismiss the value of a child's life, leave them feeling cold and fly in the face of his meticulously curated wholesome midwestern brand.

PROTECTING HEALTHCARE WORKERS

Often overlooked casualties in the battle of abortion are the medical providers who participate in these procedures. Many willing participants express regret and trauma from their involvement in aborting a child[80]. Others are forced into participating against their will. This is another group of citizens whom Walz has failed to protect.

In 2009, Cathy DeCarlo, a nurse at Mt. Sinai Hospital in New York, was forced to participate in a late-term abortion, despite her explicit objections due to her religious beliefs. The hospital threatened her, she said, with disciplinary action, including the loss of her job and license if she refused to assist in the abortion. DeCarlo later filed a legal complaint, which resulted in an HHS investigation finding that her civil rights had been violated and requiring the hospital to change its practices.

Other nurses in San Diego filed a lawsuit in 2011 after being forced to participate in abortions against their will at the University of California San Diego Medical Center. They were similarly threatened with job termination if they refused to assist in abortions. And in Illinois, the Missionary Sisters of the Sacred Heart, who operate a network of Catholic hospitals, faced pressure under state law to provide abortion services and insurance coverage for abortion. Failure to comply could result in the loss of state funding or contracts, legal penalties, and the possibility of lawsuits which would have made it difficult to provide healthcare services. For these nurses and nuns, and countless other healthcare workers, Walz did not see it fit to support any protections that came his way in Congress.

Abortion Non-Discrimination Act (H.R. 4691)

In 2012, while Walz was a congressman, he voted against the Abortion Non-Discrimination Act. This bill seeks to end discrimination against healthcare providers, medical institutions, and insurance companies that object to participating in or referring for abortions based on moral, ethical or religious beliefs. It aims to ensure that no healthcare worker is forced to participate in abortions against their will or discriminated against in hiring, and no institution can be penalized or excluded from funding for refusing to engage in abortion services.

Walz claims to value diversity and oppose discrimination in many situations, yet he supports forcing all healthcare providers to believe and do the same thing when it comes to abortion. In addition, driving healthcare providers with pro-life views out of the profession, creates a chilling effect on healthcare access in rural or religious communities.

Protect Life Act (H.R. 358)—2011

In 2011, the Protect Life Act was brought primarily to prohibit the use of federal funds for health benefits that include abortion coverage in the Affordable Care Act (Obamacare), but it also included protections for healthcare providers, allowing them to refuse to participate in abortions without facing discrimination or penalties. In keeping with his other votes that allowed for discrimination against pre-natal children based on their race or gender, Walz voted to allow discrimination against healthcare providers based on their refusal to be forced to participate in abortions against their will.[81]

PROTECTING TAXPAYERS

Another controversial aspect of Walz's pro-choice agenda is his increased funding for abortion providers. Under the Hyde Amendment, which is renewed in Congress every year, it is illegal at the federal level to use taxpayer dollars to fund abortions, but this amendment does not prohibit individual states from channeling their tax dollars toward subsidizing abortion. Walz has chosen to channel the tax dollars of his constituents toward abortion at every turn.

This broad disregard for ethical and moral considerations is a bitter pill for many to swallow. It feels like a betrayal, a sign that Walz is more interested in promoting party politics than in supporting women through the aftermath of their decisions. The money that could be spent on counseling services, adoption support, or educational programs aimed at preventing unintended pregnancies is instead funneled into expanding the reach of the very procedure they many women are pressured into or regret. But for Walz, he has taken every opportunity to pour taxpayers dollars into promoting abortion.

Protect Life Act (H.R. 358)—2011

In 2010, Tim Walz voted for the Affordable Care Act, which subsidizes health benefits with federal funding. Planned Parenthood helped shape the act.[82] Obamacare's HHS Mandate required taxpayers to fully fund abortion pills, contraceptives and sterilizations, while nearly all other medications (heart pills, insulin, etc.) received no such funding and still cost the same. Americans are required to purchase an Obamacare-compliant insurance plan or pay a heavy fine, and most individuals who are forced to purchase insurance through State Exchanges end up paying an Abortion Surcharge (Sec. 1303 Pg. 780) straight from their paychecks to fund all types of elective abortion—surgical, chemical, late term, etc. The Obamacare Secrecy Clause (Sec. 1303 (B) (3) (a) Pg. 781) states that insurance companies are not allowed to communicate in advance which plans include this abortion premium. It may only be disclosed after a person has already paid for the plan. Because this premium is taken directly from a paycheck and put directly into an abortion-on-demand fund, bypassing the tax process, it attempts to circumvent federal laws that prohibit taxpayer funding of abortion.

Obamacare uses taxpayer funding for abortions in opposition to the Hyde Amendment which makes this illegal. It accomplished this through the Abortion Premium Mandate and because Obamacare subsidizes health plans in state exchanges purchased by families of four who make $92,000 per year or less.[83] All aspects of the plan are subsidized with taxpayer dollars, including elective abortions (for plans that include it), abortion pills, contraception, etc. Therefore elective abortions are covered similarly to medical procedures, which may have a co-pay or may be subsidized completely.

In 2011, the Protect Life Act sought to prohibit the use of federal funds for health benefits that include abortion coverage in the Affordable Care Act, with exceptions for cases of rape (1% or less) or when the mother's life is endangered (less than 1%).[84] **Walz voted** for federal dollars to continue to be used to subsidize elective abortion-on-demand by voting against this act, which ultimately passed in the House by a vote of 251-175[85].

No Taxpayer Funding for Abortion Act (H.R. 3)—2011

In the same year, the No Taxpayer Funding for Abortion Act was also introduced with a goal of protecting taxpayers from paying for elective abortions through federal funding by targeting a different aspect of abortion funding and regulation. It aimed to eliminate the funding of abortion through all federal streams such as Medicaid, federal employee health benefits, and any other federal healthcare program. Again, Walz voted against this bill which sought to permanently prohibit the use of federal funds for abortion services across all federal programs, except in the 1% or less of cases of rape, or in the less than 1% of cases of life endangerment of the mother[86].

Increased Funding for Abortion

At every opportunity, Tim Walz has taken action to increase taxpayer money being funneled toward abortion. He voted for Title X family planning funds to go to organizations that perform abortions[87]. He has repeatedly voted against the Hyde Amendment in various appropriations bills, which protects federal tax dollars from funding abortion[88]. And as part of the 2019 budget he signed as governor, he increased funding abortion industry organizations in Minnesota such as Planned Parenthood, that generate as much revenue on abortion as on all the other services it provides combined. These abortion businesses are now subsidized by state taxpayer funds thanks to Walz's decisions, rather than the funding going to organizations that focus on life-affirming alternatives, such as adoption agencies and crisis pregnancy centers that do not perform abortions.

CREATING ABORTION TOURISM

In addition to removing abortion restrictions, and increasing abortion funding, Tim Walz has significantly advanced the abortion enterprise in Minnesota through his advocacy of abortion tourism. Abortion tourism is a lucrative business springing up in the wake of the Supreme Court's overturn of Roe v. Wade. Like traveling for a sporting event, which costs more than the price of the ticket, abortion tourism includes costs for hotels, meals, transportation and more, and states that profit off abortion are clamoring to bring women in for the services. Some states are generating funds by forcing taxpayers from their own states to cover the costs of abortions for women coming in from other states. Other states are profiting off the women themselves. And many states are focused on taking advantage of abortion benefits packages now being offered by certain companies that can pay $1,500 to $7,500 each time significant travel is needed for an abortion, or even $4,000 a trip, up to three times a year by some companies. These benefits include travel and lodging costs to states where abortions are legal up until the moment of birth.

Minnesota has increasingly become a destination for abortion tourism, and Tim Walz has been credited with establishing this state industry. The states surrounding Minnesota have largely created legal protections for women, children, medical workers and taxpayers that have reduced the number of abortions in their states. Alternately, as governor, Tim Walz and other state leaders have openly declared Minnesota a safe haven for abortion, causing people to flock to the state, drawn by the ease with which they can obtain an abortion.

Walz has also pledged that the state will not cooperate with investigations or prosecutions related to abortions performed within its borders. This protection from investigation includes abortions that have been performed on minors, and on women who have been sex trafficked or coerced into abortion, further solidifying its status as a destination for those seeking these services. Walz stated that his actions to advance abortion have been part of his commitment to "put up a firewall against efforts to reverse reproductive freedom," and he has played a significant role in positioning Minnesota to profit from abortion tourism through legislation, public advocacy, and executive actions[89]. In addition, his administration has supported increased funding for reproductive healthcare services, which indirectly supports the infrastructure necessary for providing abortion services to abortion tourists.

ADDITIONAL SUPPORT

Tim Walz's has not only voted for the expansion of abortion at every opportunity throughout his political career, he has lived and breathed this issue. While visiting a Battle of the Bulge memorial in 2018, intended as a solemn occasion to pay tribute to veterans and commemorate the soldiers who fought in this historic battle, Walz's focused many of his remarks on his commitment to protecting abortion rights and a woman's right to choose. He likened the battle for abortion to the historical struggle of World War II, and drew criticism for the incentive politicization of a commemorative event.

In March 2024, Governor Walz joined Vice President Harris during her visit to a St. Paul Planned Parenthood clinic, where she paid tribute to Minnesota's leadership[90]. Her office said this was the first time a president or vice president had toured a facility that performs abortions.

WRAP UP

At every turn, Walz has been a champion of abortion, willing to sacrifice anything on the altar of sexual liberty. In his 2024 Democratic National Convention speech, he proclaimed "In Minnesota, we respect our neighbors and the personal choices they make. And even if we wouldn't make those same choices for ourselves, we've got a golden rule—mind your own damn business." Walz is ordering citizens to mind their own damn business when it comes to the sexualization of children and the need for abortion that inevitably follows, and with that he has created in Minnesota a human traffickers dream.

There is literally no limit to the doors he has opened for those who want to exploit children. A nine-year-old girl could be sent into an abortion facility, cash in hand, and receive and abortion or a sterilization, and be kicked back out on the street to whoever is "acting as her parent." In Walz's world, there is no to protect that child in any way. In this area, he has created absolute liberty to the point of anarchy.

While many businesses in Minnesota have struggled to survive under Walz's governance, the one business that it is actually advantageous to be in is human trafficking. Walz's mandates require that there be no scrutiny, no monitoring, and no restrictions. And this is doubly true when the people being abused are illegal aliens. Then his policies ensure that no one's looking. But while human trafficking is flourishing in Minnesota, other businesses have been closing down.[91] It turns out Walz's command to mind your own business and respect other people's healthcare decisions doesn't apply to his orders on things like COVID.

CHAPTER 6

COVID—Endless Emergency Power

"They said there's no reason for the governor to use executive orders,"

Tim Walz said of GOP leaders after using executive orders for 15 months.

In May of 2020, COVID—19 hit the U.S. while Tim Walz was governor of Minnesota. His extended lockdowns, school and church closures, mask mandates, and restrictions on businesses and gatherings were aggressive. Under Walz's stringent approach to the pandemic, Minnesota was repeatedly ranked in the top 10 most restrictive states for COVID regulations, with a U.S. News & World Report ranking it number eight.[92]

While Minnesota was an island of authoritarian restrictiveness, it was surrounded by a sea of midwestern neighboring states with some of the least restrictions in the country. South Dakota Governor Kristi Noem stood out for taking a hands-off approach, with minimal government intervention. Wisconsin's Democrat governor repeatedly issued unilateral orders, which were then overturned by the Wisconsin Supreme Court, giving freedom to their citizens. And Iowa, Minnesota's neighbor directly to the south, was ranked the most open and free of all 50 states throughout the pandemic.

Two years of restrictive mandates, however, didn't particularly protect Minnesotans. Thirty percent of the state's population contracted COVID despite the extreme efforts Walz ordered. Iowa, conversely, with all its openness, had an infection rate of just 28%. South Dakota to the west had the same percentage of cases, about 30%, and Wisconsin to the east had only 26%. With these results, one is left to question if the cost of all the sacrifices that Walz exacted from his people can be justified by the payoff of the results.

MANDATES

For 15 months, Walz unilaterally ran the government of Minnesota by declaring a peacetime emergency and extending it 15 times. With his emergency powers, Walz issued 130 executive orders regarding COVID between March 13, 2020 and July 1, 2021. This was more than any other governor, excepting only Gavin Newsome of California who burdened his people with 150 executive orders.

In March 2020 Walz ordered that all businesses deemed "non-essential," such as small stores, restaurants, gyms, etc. be closed, and these restrictions wouldn't fully lift until 14 months later in May 2021. In July 2020 Walz issued a statewide mask mandate and social distancing protocols, requiring face coverings and distancing in all indoor public spaces and certain outdoor spaces. While many states started lifting their mask mandates altogether by February of the following year, Walz joined the more controlling states and lifted the mandate only for vaccinated individuals in May 2021, more than a year after COVID hit[93]. And Minnesota's stay at home orders under Walz were among the strictest in the country and viewed as overly authoritarian. There was significant public pushback from citizens and business owners who felt the measures were too extreme, unnecessarily strict, and an excessive use of power.[94]

These restrictions sparked protests and public dissent because the measures went too far and violated personal freedoms.[95]

Snitch on your Neighbor Hotline

Immediately following Walz's first executive orders in March 2020, he set up a COVID infraction hotline and encouraged the residents of his state to report neighbors who disobeyed any of his orders. The hotline was met with strong public opposition, as people felt uncomfortable with the notion of turning in their neighbors for relatively minor infractions, and felt Walz's pandemic response was heavy-handed and authoritarian.[96]

Many critics, particularly from conservative and libertarian groups, viewed the hotline as an example of government overreach and surveillance. The idea of encouraging citizens to report their neighbors for violating COVID restrictions was seen as fostering division and distrust within communities[97]. Civil liberties groups raised concerns that the hotline infringed on individual freedoms, as it essentially encouraged the public to police each other's behavior during a time when many people were already feeling isolated and stressed. And the hotline highlighted the difference between a dictatorial approach to compliance and the personal responsibility approach used by the leadership of many of Minnesota's neighboring states.

The public outcry grew beyond just Minnesotans to the broader nation. Florida Governor Ron DeSantis notably criticized Walz, calling the tipline a "ridiculous hotline for COVID snitches" and an example of "draconian laws."[98] He said it was another example of "government overreach," accusing Walz of encouraging Minnesotans to turn against one another over minor infractions.[99]

Walz defended his decision, stating, "We're not going to take down a phone number that people can call to keep their families safe," and in fact he kept the hotline running for two years and three months until Matt Birk, a Republican candidate for lieutenant governor, criticized the hotline on Twitter, claiming it would only continue to divide the state.[100] Three days after his original tweet, Birk reported that "Tim Walz's 'snitch line' has just now been shut down," in July of 2022.

But the snitch line wasn't taken down before 10,000 COVID-related messages passed through it. This was discovered when a Twin Cities attorney, Nathan Hansen, made a data request of the Bureau of Criminal Apprehension and redacted emails were released. These emails appear to since have been removed from their online source, but screenshots remain.[101]

Minnesotans snitched on their neighbors for things like playing basketball in a park and walking their dogs. Walz's hotline was used to alert authorities to people purchasing non-essential items at a convenience store in White Bear Lake, such as a candy bar, soda and a lottery ticket. One email said there were "too many people in Walgreens at once." A dental call center was reported for still operating, and people were reported for leaving the cities and going to their cabins. Someone else reported seeing a Facebook photo of a group of people working out at a local park in Shorewood. "I have a real problem with this and they are inviting more people to join," the person said.

A citizen of Prior Lake posted a message after the police showed up at his house.[102] His wife was dying of stage 4 lung cancer, and they had caregivers helping them fix their house for her before she died. The couple were reported to the hotline for throwing a party, and the husband had to explain to the police that they were in regular contact with these caregivers who took the necessary precautions to protect his wife from contracting COVID.

But not all emails to the hotline were complaints. One resident expressed concerns about how "completely juvenile and unnecessary" the hotline was. "We are now reporting other adults like tattling little children," the person emailed. "We don't need to be policing our peers right now and making things even more divisive towards one another." With monitoring the hotline, responding to potential infractions, and enforcing the 130 executive orders, law enforcement in the state of Minnesota was stretched thin.

Door-to-Door Vaccines

By December of 2020, the first doses of Pfizer-BioNTech vaccine were available.[103] This vaccine had been pushed through the FDA with its Emergency Use Authorization, because there had not been sufficient time to go through the normal trials and approval process.[104] Minnesota began administering the drug on December 15, 2020. As a part of Walz's public health strategy, people were sent door-to-door providing information and even offering vaccines directly at the doorstep in some areas.[105]

While Walz claimed the door-to-door campaigns were a crucial element in overcoming vaccine hesitancy and logistical barriers, they were met with backlash and negative responses from segments of the population. Many residents said that these campaigns felt invasive and amounted to government overreach.

Some people expressed discomfort with the idea of government representatives coming to homes to push vaccines, feeling pressured or coerced into making medical decisions right there on their doorstep. Others felt that having health officials and volunteers knock on their doors to promote vaccination crossed a line, especially when it came to government involvement in personal health decisions.

Some Minnesotans believed Walz's approach created a sense of pressure to get vaccinated, which might lead some to feel coerced into making a health decision they were not ready for. Others viewed the door-to-door efforts as unnecessary and a waste of resources, particularly when they felt that individuals should be responsible for their own health decisions. The campaign stirred privacy concerns, with some worrying about the government having access to personal information related to vaccination status. Political opposition also came into play. Infringement on personal liberties and freedom of choice seemed contrary to a Democratic party that normally prided itself on advocating for the right to choose.

Vaccines for Children

The "Kids Deserve a Shot" campaign was a public health initiative launched by the state of Minnesota during the COVID pandemic to push parents to get their children vaccinated. The primary goal of the campaign was to encourage vaccinations among children ages 12-17 at the time of its launch, and later ages 5–11 once the vaccines were approved for younger children.[106]

Vaccines were given out at schools, and the campaign offered monetary incentives to parents who had their children receive the full series of COVID vaccines (two doses of the Pfizer or Moderna vaccines or one dose of the Johnson & Johnson vaccine). A $200 Visa gift card was given to these families, and participants who completed their vaccinations were entered into drawings for $100,000 college scholarships.

In October 2021, Walz sent a long list of requests to the Minnesota legislature, including that they mandate student and teacher vaccinations prior to being allowed to return to school.[107] By this point, the emergency powers he had been holding onto for well over a year had been wrested from his grip. "They said there's no reason for the governor to use executive orders," Walz said of GOP leaders after using executive orders for 15 months. "I said that's fine. I trust them at their word. So I sent them a list of things they can do." Requiring vaccines was one of the things on the list.

The mortality rate for children aged 5-17 from COVID was less than 0.01% based on data from the Centers for Disease Control and Prevention (CDC) and other health authorities.[108] Most cases were either mild or asymptomatic, and even among children with severe chronic illnesses and pre-existing conditions, the overall risk remained very low. Walz said his goal with vaccinating children was to slow the spread through children to other populations, but Minnesota with all its regulations still had the same or worse percentage of COVID cases as its freer surrounding neighbors.

Critics of the "Kids Deserve a Shot" campaign raised several concerns about pushing these shots on kids. One common critique was that using financial incentives to encourage vaccinations among children could be seen as coercive or manipulative, particularly in a decision that was personal or a family choice. Others argued that the program primarily benefited families who were already inclined to vaccinate their children and would do so without the incentives.[109] Additionally, some expressed discomfort with the use of federal funding from the American Rescue Plan for what they saw as an attempt to "buy" compliance rather than focusing on education or addressing underlying concerns about vaccine hesitancy. Vaccines being offered at schools was also met with resistance. It was seen as undermining parental authority, circumventing the parental consent process, blurring the lines between education and public health, potentially pressuring students, and distracting from the schools' primary mission of educating children.

SCHOOL CLOSURES

Tim Walz's decision to close Minnesota schools for in-person learning during the COVID pandemic faced intense criticism from various sectors of the public. While the closures were intended to prevent the spread of the virus, opponents argued that the extended period of remote learning had far-reaching and long-lasting negative effects on students, particularly those from low-income and minority backgrounds.

Lengthy School Closures

Walz first ordered schools to close for in-person learning in March 2020 as the pandemic began to take hold in the state. Although some other states reopened schools in phases later that year, Minnesota's approach was more cautious. Many students in the state remained out of the classroom for large portions of the following two years. This prolonged closure caused significant learning losses and emotional strain on students. The closures disproportionately affected low-income families and children of color, exacerbating existing educational inequalities.[110]

POLITICO reported one parent's frustration with the ongoing closures, stating, "The continued lockdowns of schools have been a disaster for our kids. The governor doesn't seem to understand the long-term damage he's doing to their education and mental health." This sentiment was echoed by many parents who felt that the closures were not only unnecessary but actively harmful to their children's well-being.[111]

Decline in Student Proficiency

The educational impact of the closures was stark. Minnesota's national ranking in student proficiency dropped sharply during this period. In 2019, Minnesota was ranked 8th in the nation, but by 2021 it had fallen to 21st, and in 2023 the state was ranked 18th. Evidence over the following four years after Walz's mandates showed that less than half of Minnesota's students were proficient in reading, math or science, and many had fallen entire grade levels behind.[112]

The Minnesota Department of Education released in August 2024 the results of the Minnesota Comprehensive Assessments (MCAs) and the Minnesota Test of Academic Skills (MTAS). These results showed that only 39.5% of students met the state standards in science, 45.5% of students meet the standards in math, and 49.8% are meeting the standards in reading.

A decline in student performance was not only seen in the state of Minnesota, but the length of the school closures that Walz mandated drew particular ire. "His tyrannical thumbprint has been pressed into the development of a generation of children," said Minnesota State Representative Walter Hudson, "and he paid zero political price for it." According to the Heritage Foundation, by 2021, only 4% of Minnesota students were in districts offering a high level of in-person instruction. Walz's strict lockdowns resulted in an education system that struggled to adapt effectively to the challenges of the pandemic and failed its students. [113]

Widening Inequality

One of the most vocal criticisms of Walz's school closures centered on their disproportionate impact on vulnerable populations. Remote learning often required access to technology and reliable internet, resources that were not universally available. Low-income and minority students were hit hardest by the closures, which widened the achievement gap between them and their more affluent peers.[114] These are situations that Democrats would normally rail against, but in this case the inequity failed to raise any ire from the Left.

An analysis by the American Experiment stated that Walz's decision to shut down schools was driven by a flawed computer model that was later abandoned due to its inaccuracies. This failure, the report suggested, had catastrophic consequences for students across the state. The critics further noted that while students in Minnesota were kept out of classrooms, those in neighboring states like North Dakota experienced fewer restrictions and, according to reports, "were doing quite well."[115]

Mental Health Concerns

The mental health impact of the closures was another major point of contention.

Student mental health and test scores both suffered significantly during the pandemic. Four years later, Minnesota was only beginning to see slight improvements in graduation rates, but the damage to student well-being was already done.[116] Critics, including parents and educators, lamented that the mental health toll was an underreported consequence of the governor's decisions. A Minnesota parent quoted by POLITICO stated:" Our kids' mental health is in shambles, and Walz just doesn't seem to care."[117]

Backlash from Rural Communities

Another aspect of the controversy surrounding Walz's school closures was the backlash from rural communities. In rural Minnesota, where COVID case numbers were often lower, many parents and school administrators felt that the statewide school closures were overly broad and unnecessary. Deb Henton, executive director of the Minnesota Association of School Administrators, noted that many rural districts were frustrated by the closures, especially when they weren't experiencing significant outbreaks.[118]

The closures became a political issue, with opponents accusing Walz of prioritizing caution over common sense. They argued that local districts should have been allowed to make their own decisions about whether to stay open, based on their specific circumstances.

BUSINESS CLOSURES

During the COVID pandemic, Walz implemented a series of executive orders and restrictions that affected small businesses across the state. Small businesses are considered the backbone of many communities in Minnesota, which is made up of 70% rural area. Walz's stringent lockdowns decimated small businesses and led to economic hardships that thousands could not recover from, ending in permanent closures. The shutdown of restaurants, gyms, and other small businesses for extended periods was particularly contentious, with some claiming that the state's response caused irreparable damage to the local economy.[119]

The Minnesota Chamber of Commerce reported that by mid-2021, an estimated 5,000 to 7,000 businesses in Minnesota had closed permanently due to the pandemic. The industries most affected were hospitality, retail, and personal services, which faced some of Walz's strictest restrictions. While it is impossible to capture all the painful stories of these thousands of business owners who lost their livelihood, not to mention the tens of thousands of other businesses that suffered because of these restrictions, this is a sample of the kind of hurdles they faced.

Lisa Zarza—Alibi Drinkery and Froggy Bottoms River Pub

Lisa Zarza owned both Alibi Drinkery and Froggy Bottoms River Pub when COVID hit. At the start of the pandemic, Zarza explained that she "did everything" she was "supposed to do," in accordance with Tim Walz's mandates, but after ten months had passed, and businesses such as restaurants and bars were still shuttered, Zarza and other bar owners ended up defying Walz's shut down order.[120]

In mid-December 2020, Zarza reopened Alibi Drinkery. She was threatened with arrests and fines, and then the Attorney General's Office filed suit against Zarza for her non-compliance with the COVID shutdown orders. During the lawsuit she continued to make a living by keeping her establishment open, which led to multiple violations of executive orders. As a result of her defiance, the Minnesota Department of Public Safety and the Minnesota Department of Health revoked her liquor and food service licenses, and Zarza was then accused of operating without proper licenses. Zarza was found in contempt of court for continuing to operate her business in violation of court orders and the state's executive mandates. The courts imposed fines and further legal restrictions.

When the case was decided against her, Zarza was charged with violations of the executive orders. She faced over $300,000 in fines, including $160,000 in attorney's fees from the state's legal efforts to enforce the mandates. The court upheld the decision to revoke her licenses for five years. Zarza had to file personal bankruptcy and "leave the state to be able to legally work and make a living," she explained.[121]

Zarza pointed out repeatedly that during Walz's shutdown, places like Target, Walmart, and Home Depot had been "open 100 percent. The same exact order that shut us down, opened them all up. I think he's an evil man who overstepped his role as the governor," Zarza said of Tim Walz. "He took small businesses and ripped them up. He destroyed us."

Larvita McFarquhar—Haven's Garden

Larvita McFarquhar, the owner of Haven's Garden in Lynd, Minnesota, found herself at the center of controversy during the COVID pandemic when she defied Governor Tim Walz's executive orders mandating the closure of indoor dining. McFarquhar initially complied with the restrictions but later decided to reopen her restaurant, citing her belief that the orders were unconstitutional and infringed upon her rights. On November 27, 2020 McFarquhar hosted an indoor event at Haven's Garden, which featured food and live music, in direct violation of the state's COVID restrictions.[122]

In response to her actions, the Minnesota Department of Health and Southwest Health and Human Services (SWHHS) suspended her food license and filed a lawsuit. McFarquhar faced escalating fines, which started at $250 per day and later increased to $1,000 per day, with a total of $25,750 in fines accumulating as of early 2021.[123]

McFarquhar remained defiant, stating, "They want me to just comply... I couldn't comply with what I called unlawful and unconstitutional action by Gov. Tim Walz." She emphasized that her decision to remain open was driven by her belief in standing up for her rights and her faith.[124] McFarquhar also owned

Prestige Gymnastics and the Southwest School of Dance, both of which were also impacted by Walz's pandemic restrictions. She described the financial toll of the shutdowns, stating, "They took away everything." Despite the mounting legal pressures, McFarquhar became a symbol for those opposing the lockdowns, garnering support from groups such as the ReOpen Minnesota Coalition, which raised funds for her legal defense.[125]

Joe Holtz—Neighbors on the Rum

Joe Holtz, the owner of Neighbors on the Rum in Princeton, Minnesota, became one of several bar and restaurant owners who defied Governor Tim Walz's executive orders prohibiting indoor dining during the COVID pandemic. Holtz reopened his restaurant in December 2020 despite the ongoing restrictions, citing his desire to support his employees during the holiday season. He explained that he implemented safety precautions, including mask-wearing and additional sanitizing, but felt compelled to open to provide his workers with the opportunity to make a living.[126]

Holtz faced significant consequences for his actions. State health inspectors, accompanied by police, shut down his establishment, and the Minnesota Attorney General's office took legal action against him. His liquor license was suspended for two months as a result of his defiance. Holtz remained defiant, stating," We're safe people...We do everything in our possible creation right, and you tell me I can't let my people make money. You're going to take livelihoods away from people at Christmas time?" Holtz made it clear that his decision was driven by the financial well-being of his employees, one of whom earned $1,200 in tips the night they reopened, which he planned to match out of his own pocket.[127]

Holtz's involvement with the ReOpen Minnesota Coalition highlighted his belief in standing up against what he saw as unfair restrictions. Though his business was closed down by state authorities, Holtz's stance was rooted in his commitment to his employees and his frustration with the continued restrictions that were forcing many businesses like his to the brink of closure.[128]

Thousands More

There are thousands of others like Lisa Zarza, Larvita McFarquhar, and Joe Holtz. While there is no way to capture all their stories and the pain that the controlling and fearful approach Walz took to the COVID lockdowns inflicted on so many people, this is a high-level picture of a few more.

Gandolfi Fish Market, owned by the Gandolfi sisters was a beloved fish market that operated for decades. It closed its doors after Walz's extended shutdowns harmed not only dining establishments, but also the tourism industry.[129]

Modern Times Café, owned by Theresa Shea, was a Minneapolis café known for its vegetarian fare. Theresa was unable to recover from the economic impact of the COVID restrictions, with the prolonged shutdowns and limited seating capacities making it impossible.[130]

Pumphouse Creamery, owned by Barb Zapzalka was a favorite local ice cream shop in south Minneapolis, but it couldn't withstand the pandemic-related restrictions. The financial toll of Walz's orders led to its closure.[131]

Tandem Bagels, owned by Marty and Nancy Newton, was located in Mankato. This family-owned bagel shop closed permanently after facing mounting financial losses. The Newtons cited the state's lockdown policies as a major factor in their inability to stay open.[132]

Black Coffin Tattoo, owned by Zachary Pearson was a tattoo parlor in Minneapolis that struggled to stay open during the shutdowns. The forced closure and slow reopening schedule made it impossible for Pearson to keep the business going.[133]

As business owners tried to balance financial survival against compliance with Walz's mandates, many of them lost their livelihoods. Over 150 businesses formed the Reopen Minnesota Coalition, urging the governor to lift restrictions. Walz, however, stood firm as one business after another shuttered its doors and hung up "Sorry, We're Permanently Closed" signs. One critic called his policies "one of the biggest assaults on our liberties in our lifetime."[134]

As businesses were forced to shut down, the state's unemployment numbers surged.[135] The Minnesota Unemployment Insurance system was overwhelmed by the number of claims as these shutdowns continued. While demand grew, people who needed help found that the system was poorly managed and slow in processing claims, leaving many residents without timely financial support.[136] Delays in unemployment payments further frustrated business owners who were used to providing for themselves but were left struggling to make ends meet.[137] Kara Lovemelt, owner of an interactive videography and photography business said, "We went from thriving to diving in a matter of a day."[138]

CHURCH CLOSURES

During the COVID pandemic, Governor Tim Walz faced substantial backlash for his handling of church closures in Minnesota. The measures he implemented, aimed at curbing the spread of the virus, led to significant tension between the state government and religious communities. While other establishments such as retail stores, restaurants, and even casinos were eventually allowed to reopen under certain guidelines, churches remained under stricter regulations for extended periods, leading to accusations of religious discrimination and constitutional violations.

Timeline of Church Closures and Restrictions

In March 2020, as COVID cases began rising in Minnesota, Governor Walz issued an executive order that closed places of worship along with other public gathering spaces. This was in line with the state's stay-at-home order that required nonessential businesses to close temporarily. Initially, most religious leaders complied with the closure orders. However, frustration mounted as churches remained closed or under heavy restrictions even as other sectors of the economy began reopening.

A key moment of contention arose in May 2020, when Walz allowed retail stores and malls to reopen at 50% capacity, while limiting churches to gatherings of no more than 10 people. This discrepancy sparked understandable outrage among religious leaders and communities, who argued that they were being unfairly targeted compared to secular institutions. The Star Tribune reported that two churches and a group of businesses filed a federal lawsuit challenging Walz's orders, accusing the state of unfairly picking "winners and losers" by allowing certain businesses to reopen while keeping churches closed.[139]

Legal Battles and Lawsuits

Several religious organizations filed lawsuits against the Walz administration, claiming that the restrictions on religious gatherings violated their First Amendment rights. One such lawsuit was filed in August 2020 by Cornerstone Church of Alexandria, Life Spring Church, and Calvary Chapel. The plaintiffs argued that Walz's orders were unconstitutional, stating that the executive orders "criminalize the conduct of church attendees, suppress plaintiffs' ability to worship and practice their religion in houses of worship, and restrict the ability of the plaintiffs to associate with other members of the faith."[140]

These lawsuits garnered national attention, with religious liberty organizations such as the Thomas More Society and Liberty Counsel stepping in to represent the churches. Erick Kaardal, special counsel with the Thomas More Society, criticized the governor's handling of the situation, stating: "One of the things we will remember about the Minnesota governor's response to fear of COVID is the unconstitutional, discriminatory treatment of churches and synagogues."[141] This sentiment was echoed by many religious leaders who felt that their constitutional rights were being sidelined in the name of public health.

Prolonged Restrictions and Public Outcry

While restrictions on businesses gradually eased, places of worship remained under tight regulations. For months, religious leaders pressed for a loosening of the rules, emphasizing that faith was an essential aspect of life that could not be equated with nonessential activities like shopping or dining out. In May 2020, the Lutheran Church-Missouri Synod and the Archdiocese of St. Paul and Minneapolis publicly declared their intent to defy the governor's restrictions, asserting their right to resume in-person worship services.[142]

The issue reached a national scale when President Donald Trump declared houses of worship essential and threatened to override state governors who refused to allow churches to reopen. This put additional pressure on Walz, who eventually partially conceded, allowing places of worship to reopen at 25% capacity while maintaining strict social distancing.

WRAP UP

Walz received significant criticism for his use of executive orders to implement COVID restrictions in Minnesota. His extensive government mandates and control over business operations reflected socialist principles, and his emphasis on state intervention and control aligned with Marxist ideals. Republican lawmakers saw his extended use of emergency powers as bypassing the normal legislative process, and that making decisions with such significant economic and social impacts should have been debated and passed through the legislature rather than enacted unilaterally.[143]

Groups filed lawsuits challenging the legality of Walz's emergency orders. They argued that Walz's prolonged use of emergency powers without legislative involvement violated the separation of powers as laid out in the Minnesota Constitution.

Republican lawmakers introduced bills to limit the governor's power to extend emergency declarations without legislative consent, but unsurprisingly, these efforts were blocked by the Democratic-controlled House. The ongoing ability of the Democrat leader of the state of Minnesota to issue any order he wanted for more than a year put the Democratic party in a tremendously powerful position to advance their agendas under the guise of an ongoing state of emergency.

Perhaps because they recognized that Walz would never voluntarily give up dictatorial power once he had it, the Democrats finally agreed to revoke Walz's ability to continue his ongoing declarations of a state of emergency. A budget deal, which would only pass in the Republican-controlled senate if the Democrats agreed to break Walz's stranglehold on the government, was passed on June 30, 2021, ending the supreme command of Walz's COVID rule.

While Walz was criticized for functioning as a dictator who was unwilling to let go of total authority, and for being oppressive and slow in lifting restrictions, particularly in comparison to neighboring states, public protests broke out. Driven by frustration over his strict business closures, mask mandates, and limits on social gatherings, protests attracted a mix of business owners, workers, and individuals advocating for personal freedom. They gathered at prominent public locations, demanding an end to lockdown measures. Hundreds of protesters gathered at the State Capitol carrying signs saying, "End the Shutdown" and "Reopen Minnesota." Other protests took the form of car rallies or "gridlock" protests. Participants drove through the streets of St. Paul and other cities, honking horns, waving flags, and holding signs. Citizens also protested wearing face coverings, seeing them as an infringement on personal freedom and bodily autonomy, a topic which was so dear to Walz when it came to other issues like abortion.

While protestors rallied against "government overreach," law enforcement was dispatched to maintain order and prevent mandate infractions. On top of doing their actual job and dealing with the COVID mandates in their own lives, law enforcement officers were stretched even thinner trying to handle the mounting unrest stirred up by Walz's lockdowns.

CHAPTER 7

Race Riots—Politically Driven

"The elections were coming up and everything was politically driven. They were going to use this incident for a political narrative, and they did."

—Minneapolis Police Officer[144]

During the spring of 2020, while Minnesota was already in the throes of the COVID-19 pandemic, with widespread government-mandated lockdowns, business closures, and economic hardships, Minnesotans were grappling with job losses, isolation, and uncertainty. The economic toll from COVID, especially on vulnerable populations, exacerbated social unrest, and tensions ran high with protests outside the State Capitol, neighbors snitching on each other, and business owners watching as their livelihoods slipped through their fingers.[145] As the financial and psychological pain increased, law enforcement in

Minnesota was under significant strain trying to manage the unrest while also enforcing Walz's lockdown policies. These conditions created a backdrop of widespread frustration and anxiety that preceded the explosive reactions to the death of George Floyd.

LAW ENFORCEMENT STRETCHED THIN

Law enforcement officers, like everyone else, were impacted by the pandemic. But in addition to pressure to follow Walz's orders for themselves, they were also in charge of making sure that every other citizen was following his restrictions.

Enforcing Lockdowns and COVID Mandates

Curfews, limits on gatherings, business closures, and mask mandates were just a few of Walz's mandates which required policing to ensure compliance. Police officers were tasked with enforcing social distancing regulations, ensuring compliance with stay-at-home orders, managing violations of public health mandates, and monitoring reports that citizens made on their neighbors. They also had to respond to reports that came through Walz's snitch hotline. This effectively doubled their workload. There were still responsible for handling issues like domestic violence, keeping the roads safe, and preventing crime, while simultaneously being expected to enforce Walz's pandemic-related orders.[146]

Monitoring Public Spaces

As public spaces, including parks and beaches, were subject to Walz's crowd control measures, law enforcement officers had to be vigilant in ensuring that gatherings did not exceed government-imposed limits. This meant that they had to have eyes everywhere at once, looking for lawbreakers in places that were typically peaceful and among people who were generally law-abiding. This stretched their resources further, as they were required to disperse crowds and enforce restrictions across urban, suburban and rural areas.[147]

Increased Public Tension

The stress of the pandemic contributed to heightened emotions and increased interactions between the public and law enforcement, particularly regarding COVID-related enforcement. Eventually citizens began to protest the extreme measures being taken in the name of public safety. Eventually law enforcement, forced at times to uphold policies not all officers supported, was dispatched to confront protesters. These dynamics left officers dealing with both compliance enforcement and public dissent (Fox Business) (Star Tribune).

Operational Changes Due to COVID

Law enforcement agencies were also managing the internal impacts of the pandemic. Officers had to adapt to new protocols, such as maintaining their own health, handling COVID-positive detainees, and dealing with staff shortages due to illness or quarantine. These factors reduced the number of available personnel to respond to both everyday policing and the rising civil unrest (Star Tribune).

The combination of these factors meant that law enforcement agencies were already operating at reduced capacity and heightened stress levels by May of 2020.

BACKGROUND ON GEORGE FLOYD

In 2014, six years before COVID descended on Minnesota, George Floyd took a Greyhound bus from Huston to Minneapolis looking for a new life. He would end up becoming a flashpoint for a city whose fuse had grown short, but few know the events of his life that preceded this spark.

Early Life

Born in North Carolina in 1973, Floyd moved to Texas at age three when his parents separated, where he moved with his mother and siblings into a Cuney Homes housing project in Houston's historically Black Third Ward. Growing up in one of the poorest sections of the city, he pursued athletics as the best way to escape his circumstances, and was accepted into community college and then Texas A&M. But unable to meet the school's academic requirements, Floyd eventually dropped out and returned to his family's home where he became involved in the local hip-hop scene.[148]

Drug Use and Criminal History

George Floyd struggled with drug addiction throughout his life, which he openly acknowledged. He was reported to have used various substances, including opioids and fentanyl.

At 24 years of age, Floyd's record of criminal activities began, and continued through until his death. He was charged with crimes under his name, as well as four known aliases, including Perry Floyd and Omar Jamal Kett.[149]

> **1997**—Convicted of felony for drug possession in Texas and served six months in county jail[150]
>
> **1998**—Convicted of felony under the name Omar Jamal Kett for aggravated robbery of Juan Botello with a firearm and served 10 months in prison[151]
>
> **1998**—Convicted of misdemeanor for theft and served 10 days in county jail

2001—Convicted of misdemeanor for trespassing and served 30 days in jail[152]

2002—Convicted of felony for possession of cocaine and served eight months in prison

2004—Convicted of felony for delivery of cocaine and served 10 months in prison

2005—Convicted of felony for possession of cocaine with intent to deliver and served 10 months in state jail

2007—Convicted of felony for aggravated robbery with a deadly weapon, after entering a pregnant woman's home in Houston, holding a gun to her abdomen, and searching for drugs and money, was sentenced to five years in state prison in 2009 as part of a plea deal and was released in 2013

2019—Arrested for a narcotics violation for having a large amount of OxyContin

During the 2019 arrest, George Floyd was a passenger during a traffic stop. The arrest report stated that Floyd was acting suspiciously, and upon investigation, officers found a large amount of drugs in the vehicle. According to his own admission, Floyd swallowed a significant number of pills before being arrested. When the officers told him to show his hands and then step out of the car, he resisted repeatedly, hiding his hands and trying to hide drugs. He was reportedly uncooperative and resistant to instructions, instead talking about how he just lost his mother, and saying over and over, "Please don't shoot me." After Floyd admitted to police officers that he had swallowed pills, the officers called paramedics. They found Floyd's blood pressure was very high and took him to the hospital. Had Floyd not admitted the drug use, paramedics might not have been called, which could have resulted in Floyd having a heart attack. The 2019 arrest of George Floyd did not lead to a conviction.[153]

ARREST AND DEATH OF GEORGE FLOYD

For about five years, the majority of the time George Floyd was in Minneapolis, he worked as a security guard at Conga Latin Bistro. He lived with a roommate he met in a drug rehab program and appears to have stayed out of criminal activity during much of that time. Then one day he found his roommate dead in their home from an overdose, which took Floyd to a dark place set him on a course to relapse.[154] In March of 2020, because of Walz's strict lockdown orders, Floyd was laid off from his job. The loss of his employment lead to financial difficulties.[155]

On May 25, 2020, George Floyd went to the convenience store Cup Foods in the Powderhorn Park neighborhood where a store clerk called the police to report that Floyd used counterfeit $20 bills to purchase cigarettes. The man "is awfully drunk," the clerk reported, "and he's not in control of himself."[156]

Minneapolis police officers Thomas Lane and J. Alexander Kueng were the first to arrive on the scene around 8 pm. Floyd was sitting in a nearby car with two other people when Lane approached. According to the body cam footage, the officers attempted to arrest Floyd and bring him to their patrol car as Floyd resisted at each step.[157]

- Officer Lane approached the car where Floyd was sitting in the driver's seat. Officer Lane told Floyd to show his hands 16 times as Floyd ignored the officer's orders and kept his hands out of view moving around in the car. Officer Lane drew his gun, and Floyd continued to keep his hands out of view, even after the gun was drawn.

- Body cam video showed what looked like pills in Floyd's mouth.
- Officer Lane told Floyd to step out of the car eight times. As Floyd ignored the officer's orders, Shawanda Hill, Floyd's friend sitting in the back seat yelled, "Stop resisting, Floyd." Officer Kueng told Floyd, "Stop resisting, man."
- The officers told Floyd to stand up out of his car five times as Floyd repeatedly ignored their orders. One officer told Floyd to walk with him three times and to sit down four times before Floyd sat against a nearby building wall.
- Floyd cried, "Please, I don't want to go back there," and said he was shot last time he was arrested, which was not true.
- Officer Kueng, who is Black asked, "Do you know why we're here? We're here because it sounds like you gave a fake bill to the individuals in there. And do you know why we pulled you out of the car? Because you was [sic] not listening to anything we told you."
- Officers Lane and Kueng asked, "Are you on something man? Cause you're acting all erratic." Floyd responded, "I'm not, no nothing." Officer said, "You've got foam around your mouth too." Shawanda Hill also told Officer Land that Floyd wasn't on any drugs.
- Officers Derek Chauvin and Tou Thao arrived shortly after to assist.

- Officers said, “Stop moving around,” “Stop falling down,” “Stand up,” “Stay on your feet and face the car door,” “Face the door,” “Face the door, “Stand up straight,” and “Sit still,” as Floyd screamed, “Please,” and “I’m not that kind of guy,” over and over and physically resisted every attempt to have him sit in the back seat of the police SUV.
- Floyd made many statements about being claustrophobic, not being able to breathe, having anxiety and wanting to have his hands released. He said, “When I start breathing, when I start breathing it’s going to go off on me,” “My breathing’s going to go off on me man,” and “I can’t choke, I can’t breathe while in the back of the squad SUV.” “I’m going to die in there.” He repeatedly said, “I just had COVID; I can’t breathe.” “I’ll go on the ground, anything.”
- An officer pulled a marijuana pipe from Floyd’s pocket.
- Floyd said, “Please stay with me,” several times to one of the officers, who said, “I will.”
- Floyd repeatedly indicated that he wanted to have his handcuffs taken off. He said, “I just want my hands free. I won’t do nothing to you all man. And I understand that people do stuff, and you all don’t know me,” and “I’m claustrophobic, I’ve got anxiety, I don’t want to do anything to them.” Floyd also asked to sit in the front seat.
- Both back doors of the SUV were open, and an officer said, “I’ll roll the windows down” four times and “I’ll turn the air on.”

- Officers told Floyd to get in the car seven times and to take a seat 11 times as he bodily resisted, throwing himself on the ground, and at one point on the floor of the car, then pushing his way out the other door.
- Floyd repeatedly screamed, "Please," and "I'm not a bad guy" while bodily flailing around in the back of the SUV, and screamed over and over, "I can't breathe," while officers were only touching his legs.
- Floyd said "I want to lay on the ground" five different times in extreme agitation while in the back of the SUV and while pushing his way out the other door and physically resisting at an extreme level.
- A bystander yelled to Floyd, "You're gonna die of a heart attack, man! Get in the car."
- An officer asked if Floyd was going to jail. Officer Kueng who is Black, said, "He's under arrest right now for forgery, but we don't know what's going on."
- The officers decided to take Floyd out of the SUV because he was violently throwing himself around and wouldn't remain seated. One told him to "Come on out." Floyd said, "Thank you" several times.
- While lying on the ground, Floyd tried to kick Officer Lane repeatedly.
- Officers used Maximal Restraint Technique as depicted in words and drawings in policy 5-316 of the Minneapolis Police Department manual, including use of a hobble to stop Floyd from kicking, use of a knee against the side of Floyd's neck to stop him from moving around, and two officers holding him at his back and legs. The Maximal Restraint Technique re-

quired that officers monitor the restrained subject until the arrival of medical personnel.[158]

- 36 seconds after Floyd was on the ground, Officer Lane called for an EMS ambulance, Code 2, which requires immediate response without lights or sirens.
- Floyd continued to talk while he was restrained on the ground. He said he couldn't breathe more than 10 additional times, like he had said 1) before he got into the squad SUV, 2) while he was in the back of the squad SUV, and 3) while he was on the ground before he was restrained. He also called for his mother and said he loved several people. He said, "I can't breathe; it's COVID, man" and talked several times about his face being gone. Officers told him he sounded fine and that he should relax and take deep breaths.
- Officer Chauvin asked Floyd what he wanted. Floyd responded, "Please, I can't breathe." Officer Chauvin told him to get up and get in the car four times. Floyd said he would, but he couldn't move. Chauvin continued to apply the Maximal Restraint Technique.
- While restrained on the ground Floyd stopped struggling and appeared to pass out, with what appeared to be foam around his mouth.
- Bystanders urged officers to stop restraining him because he couldn't breathe. Officers took Floyd's pulse and increased the EMS call to Code 3, which requires the use of lights and siren. Officers continued to restrain Floyd until the EMS ambulance arrived. Once EMS had gotten the stretcher ready, they cleared the

officers to release the restraints on Floyd, and the officers stopped using the Maximal Restraint Technique.

- Officer Lane went in the ambulance to offer to help. Body cam video showed that oxygen tubing being used was not connected to an oxygen source. It also showed him giving chest compressions to revive Floyd.[159]
- Floyd went into cardiac arrest in the ambulance and was later pronounced dead at Hennepin County Medical Center.[160]

AUTOPSY

After the arrest, pills containing methamphetamine and fentanyl were recovered from the vehicle Floyd was in. More pills with his saliva and DNA were recovered from the back of the police squad SUV. These were consistent with Floyd's words and actions, what was seen on the body cam video, and what was found in the autopsy.

Official Autopsy

On May 26, 12 hours after George Floyd's death, an autopsy was conducted by Hennepin County Medical Examiner Dr. Andrew M Baker. Amy Sweasy Tamburino, a senior prosecutor who would eventually prosecute the officers involved, asked him to do the autopsy early that morning. The report he produced was based on an autopsy examination of George Floyd's body, and toxicology results from blood, urine and other samples. He did not watch any videos of George Floyd prior to conducting the autopsy. Later that day he met with prosecutors and FBI officials where his report revealed that Floyd did not have any life-threatening injuries and had died of cardiac arrest. Three major findings from his report were:

1) There was no visible evidence Floyd died of asphyxiation or strangulation. There was no bruising on his neck and no bruises on his back or evidence of blunt trauma. There were no signs of damage to his airways.

2) Floyd had two types of heart disease, Hypertensive Heart Disease and Coronary Artery Disease. One of his arteries was 75% blocked. He also had COVID.

3) Significant levels of Fentanyl, methamphetamine, THC cotinine and other drugs were in his system.

The report also stated, "Most cases of untreated hypertension," (which is known as "the silent killer") "can put you at risk for death." The report continues, "Certain intoxicants can exacerbate and increase the risk of death." One of the symptoms of a fentanyl overdose is slow or no breathing. Floyd's fentanyl level was at 11 ng/ml. "Deaths have been certified w/ levels of 3," Baker reported. "If he were found dead at home alone and no other apparent causes, this could be acceptable to call an OD (overdose)." Mixing fentanyl with other drugs increases the likelihood of a fatal interaction. Difficulty breathing is also a common symptom for both of Floyd's heart diseases, both of which have higher risks for COVID-19 complications. The official autopsy report also listed cotinine in Floyd's system, which forms when nicotine from tobacco smoke enters the body. This incident started because George Floyd bought cigarettes with counterfeit money. The CDC also listed smoking as a higher risk for severe COVID complications.

This official autopsy was conducted before the rioting and the looting in Minneapolis started. The results, however, were not released until June 1, 2020, a week after the autopsy was conducted. When the report was released, it forced the media, the left and everybody else to make a tough decision. Either they could admit they jumped to conclusions, or they could insist their narrative of racist policing was right and the autopsy was wrong. Although with the circling of the cancel culture vultures, few were willing to admit they had jumped to conclusions about anything.

Newsweek, however noted, "The preliminary findings in the Hennepin County medical examiner's autopsy of Floyd revealed no physical findings that support a diagnosis of traumatic asphyxia or strangulation." The article went on to point out something that was often overlooked in the videos. "George Floyd could not breathe prior to his restraint."

The official autopsy revealed that Floyd couldn't have died from his neck being crushed by Derrick Chauvin's knee because there were no signs of traumatic asphyxia or strangulation, or other life-threatening injuries to his neck or throat. After seeing the body cam videos, Dr. Baker said, "From the videos I have seen, it appears like his (Officer Chauvin's) knee is on the side of his neck, not where the structures are" in his respiratory system.[161]

Amy Sweasy Tamburino later testified that Baker called her the day of the autopsy to tell her there were "no medical findings that showed any injury to the vital structures of Mr. Floyd's neck. There were no medical indications of asphyxia or strangulation." She also testified that he said, "Amy, what happens when the evidence doesn't match up with the public narrative that everyone's already decided on?" And then he said, "This is the kind of case that ends careers."

After Baker's report was released, he received hundreds of death threats.[162] Baker later testified in court that George Floyd's death was a result of the combination of several factors, including the stress of the interaction with the police, his underlying heart disease, and the presence of drugs in his system.

Floyd Family Autopsy Review

George Floyd's family commissioned two doctors, Dr. Michael Baden and Dr. Allecia Wilson to review the viral video and provide and autopsy with their opinion of what lead to Floyd's death. This review did not include a toxicology report. It was often referred to as an independent autopsy review, however, the review came about because the doctors were hired by Floyd's family.[163]

The autopsy review reported that George Floyd's death was due to "asphyxiation from sustained pressure" and ruled the manner of death as homicide. The report did not mention that Floyd had COVID, heart diseases or was using drugs. It did not explain why Floyd said, "I can't breathe. The doctors apparently disputed that Floyd died of cardiac arrest. They also implied that no other conditions or factors contributed to his death. The report stated, "What those officers did as we have seen on the video is his cause of death, not some underlying unknown health condition. George Floyd was a healthy young man. George died because he needed a breath. He needed a breath of air."[164]

The official autopsy report was withheld from the public until June 1, 2020. It was on this same day that the Floyd family autopsy review was released, and Ben Crump, the civil rights attorney who represented the Floyd family, repeatedly announced that George Floyd was a healthy young man with no underlying medical conditions that contributed to his death.[165]

GOVERNMENT RESPONSE AND RIOTS

Walz's and other government officials' response to the arrest and death of George Floyd played a significant role in creating and escalating Black Lives Matter riots and the destruction of Minneapolis and other areas. The use of racially charged language by government leaders within hours of Floyd's death created narratives that were not supported by due process, or any adherence to the integrity of the legal system, or any adherence to the fundamental right of innocence until proven guilty.

May 26, 2020

- **Official Autopsy Conducted**: An official autopsy on George Floyd was conducted less than 12 hours after his death. The results were withheld from the public for six days, until June 1.
- **Calls for Bodycam Footage**: Public demands for the release of the bodycam footage began almost immediately. Despite previous pushes for transparency, particularly following the Fergusen riots which called for all police officers to be equipped with body cams, the footage was withheld for 70 days, until August 3.
- **Frey Fired Officers Without Due Process**: At 3:09 p.m., less than 24 hours after the arrest and death of George Floyd, Mayor Jacob Frey tweeted that the four officers involved in Floyd's arrest were terminated. The officers were fired without due process, and Frey suggested their actions were racially motivated by stating, "Being Black in America should not be a death sentence." This statement likely inflamed public sentiment against the officers, including Officer J. Al-

exander Kueng, who was Black, and was in keeping with Frey's previous decisions against police officers for perceived racial offenses without due process.[166]

- **BLM Protests Escalated**: Black Lives Matter organized protests that began in the afternoon, and by evening, they escalated into riots, with looting, vandalism, and arson.[167] The Third Precinct police station was vandalized with graffiti and smashed windows. Police officers used tear gas and rubber bullets to disperse the violent crowds.
- **Occupation of George Floyd Square**: Black Lives Matter protestors took over several city blocks at the intersection of 38th Street and Chicago Avenue and turned it into an autonomous zone without police presence.
- **Walz's Primal Scream Statement**: Walz said in a press conference he shared the "urge of just a primal scream" watching the bystander video, and that protesting is "how people express their pain, process tragedy and work to create change." "I would encourage them to do so with a mask, to socially distance," he said. "We certainly don't want to see things turn violent in any way, but I also think this is a pretty normal response."[168]
- **Police Were Told Not to Intervene**: Police officers reported difficulties in receiving clear orders from command, often getting no response when they called. When orders were given, they were told not to stop the vandalism and looting and to avoid wearing riot gear, even as they were pelted with rocks, frozen water bottles, and bricks by rioters. Two people were

stabbed during the riots with one dying. The media, however, did not cover their stories or names. Residents, fearing for their safety and their property, slept on their porches with baseball bats or anything they could find to protect their homes.

May 27, 2020

- Continued Rioting: Riots continued, with Black Lives Matter rioters looting stores like a local Target, where they used claw hammers to smash open cash registers. Police were ordered not to interfere, but just to observe and report. Rioters set fire to an AutoZone and other businesses. Police were told not to stop the vandalism or looting. Firemen were sent to stop the blaze at AutoZone, which was burning toxic chemicals. Rioters attacked the firefighters, and police officers made a wall around them with their bodies, still not permitted to wear riot gear.
- Police Injuries Reported: Reports emerged of police officers being injured by projectiles thrown by rioters, including rocks and bricks. The increasing violence against law enforcement led to calls for additional support.
- Walz's Solidarity Statement: At a press conference in the afternoon Walz thanked the protesters and said, "Our heart and our solidarity are with folks who understand Monday night what happened to George Floyd." He added that he was "saddened" that some of the protestors were in harm's way the prior night and encouraged everyone to be safe.[169]

- Verbal Request for National Guard Assistance: At 6:23 p.m., Minneapolis Police Chief Arradondo called Mayor Frey, requesting National Guard assistance due to the overwhelming situation.[170] Frey called Governor Walz, who was reportedly noncommittal about sending in the Guard, saying "he would consider" sending in troops.[171] Frey later told newspapers that the phone conversation with Walz was a formal request for National Guard support. Walz and his office countered that it wasn't. At 9:11 p.m., Arradondo also forwarded an email, from MPD Commander Scott Gerlicher to John Harrington, the state's public safety commissioner including a document with the outline of a plan asking for 600 National Guard troops.[172]
- Inadequate Direction from City Leadership: As the chaos grew, clear leadership and decisive action were lacking. Rioters continued to loot and set fires throughout the night. Police reported that they were still being "hit with rocks and frozen water bottles, and being shot at with mortars." They asked if they could escalate their use of force to deploy SKAT tear gas rounds. They were told "negative" by command.[173]
- Large-Scale Arson: Rioters began large-scale arson, setting fires to buildings, businesses, restaurants, stores, and vehicles causing hundreds of millions of dollars in property damage across the city.

May 28, 2020

- **Frey's Statement on Public Anger**: In a press conference, Frey said, "If you're feeling that sadness, that anger, it's not only understandable, it's right."
- **Distributing Masks**: Frey ordered masks to be handed out to rioters in an effort to mitigate the spread of the virus while acknowledging the right of individuals to protest and exercise free expression. This decision came just three days after he announced he was considering an emergency regulation to prevent churches in Minneapolis from being allowed to gather at 25% capacity as was beginning around the state.[174]
- **Written Formal Request for the National Guard**: At 10:55 a.m., Frey submitted a formal written request for National Guard assistance.[175] He also issued a local emergency declaration.[176] At 12:23 p.m., Arradondo also sent an e-mail including a list of "critical infrastructure sites to be protected," listing the five police precinct headquarters and other government and medical buildings and businesses along Lake Street and other areas.
- **Small Mobilization of the National Guard**: In the afternoon, at about 2:30 p.m., almost four hours after Frey's request, Walz issued an executive order activating a limited number of his state's National Guard.[177] The executive order said that Frey and St. Paul Mayor Melvin Carter both requested assistance "to help provide security and restore safety."
- **Third Precinct Abandoned to Rioters**: A Minneapolis Police Seargent said she listened as Wals said, "Give

it up," of the Third Precinct, and Mayor Frey made the decision that police officers should abandon the station in what appeared to be a prize or appeasement to rioters.[178] Police officers were ordered to load the station's weapons, gear and other items into a bus that came to the back door. They were also told to take down the cameras. Hours later when the officers were ordered to evacuate, they were made to run a gauntlet through thousands of Black Lives Matter rioters who threw projectiles at them to a bus that was supposed to meet them half a mile away. The bus was late. The precinct was set on fire, along with several nearby structures, symbolizing the city's loss of control over the situation. This was seen as a sign of weakness and a failure to protect public property and maintain order.

- **Confidential Information Leaked**: At 10:31 p.m., Tim Walz's 19-year-old daughter Hope, tweeted confidential information about law enforcement's plans.[179] "Could someone who actually has followers rely [sic] to the masses that have gotten 'national guard' trending that the guard WILL NOT be present tonight??" "The guard can not [sic] be sent in within minutes," she added in one of several posts, noting that "it takes time for them to deploy because they come from all over the state."
- **Deployment of National Guard**: At 11:41 p.m., the guard tweeted that it had "activated more than 500 soldiers to St. Paul, Minneapolis and surrounding communities," but at that time only 90 soldiers were on the ground.[180]

- **Continued Destruction**: Police officers described the riots as a modern-day war time situation with Black Lives Matter rioters continuing to throw bricks and rocks, light roman candles and Molotov cocktails, smash steel bars through store windows and set fire to cars and buildings. Police were still directed not to wear riot gear so as not to look militant.

May 29, 2020

- **Presidential Pressure**: President Trump created pressure for Walz to get the situation under control. He considered using the Insurrection Act of 1807 that allows the President to deploy federal military forces within the United States to suppress civil disorder, insurrection, or rebellion if state and local authorities were unable or unwilling to do so, as was done in the 1960s desegregation of schools and the 1992 L.A. Riots. At 12:53 a.m., President Trump tweeted that the very weak Radical Left Mayor, Jacob Frey, needed to get his act together and bring the city under control or he would send in the National Guard. He also said he had spoken with Governor Tim Walz and offered federal military assistance to restore order. Walz refused Trump's offer to bring in the military.[181]
- **Failed Attempt to Reclaim Precinct**: Walz gave the order to have law enforcement reclaim the Third Precinct after an estimated $10 million of damage was done. Efforts to regain control of the area were met with ongoing chaos and the precinct was never reoccupied by police.

- **Abject Failure**: That morning, Walz had a private phone call with Frey and others in the Third Precinct and gave no indication that he was about to publicly rebuke Minneapolis' response to the riots. Then amid criticism after one of the most destructive nights in Minneapolis history, Walz stood outside the smoldering Third Precinct police station and accused Frey of losing control of his city, calling the response an "abject failure."[182]
- **Chauvin Arrested**: In the afternoon, Derek Chauvin was arrested and charged with third-degree murder and second-degree manslaughter.
- **Limited Mobilization of the National Guard**: Walz issued another executive order to increase the National Guard to 700 soldiers on duty.
- **Curfew Ignored**: Walz ordered an 8 p.m. curfew for the first night in Minneapolis and St. Paul, which went largely unenforced, and rioting continued in both cities.[183]

May 30, 2020

- **More Violent BLM Protests**: Black Lives Matter organized protests in cities around the nation that erupted in violence, breaking windows, attacks on police officers, and lighting cars on fire.
- **Walz Statement About Protests**: Walz stated in a press conference, "It started with the tragic and senseless murder of George Floyd, and it extended through

the week of righteous anger being expressed by community leaders and all people of conscience."

- **Walz Family Evacuation**: Walz expressed his concerns about protesters who gathered outside his residence in St. Paul with an upside-down American flag, a distress signal symbolizing the dire state of affairs and the perceived threat to life and property. Walz had his family evacuated from the residence.
- **Full Mobilization of the National Guard**: Three days after the initial request for assistance, Governor Walz ordered a full mobilization of the National Guard. In a post at 10:33 p.m., the Guard wrote, "We now have more than 4,100—quickly moving toward 10,800—Minnesota Citizen-Soldiers and Airmen supporting our friends and neighbors in the Twin Cities."[184] The full mobilization came after much of the damage had already been done.

June 1, 2020

- **Autopsy Reports**: The official autopsy report was made public six days after being conducted, along with the autopsy review commissioned by the family of George Floyd.
- **Posting Bail**: Kamala Harris tweeted, "If you're able to, chip in now to the @MNFreedomFund to help post bail for those protesting on the ground in Minnesota."[185] That endorsement helped the Minnesota Freedom Fund raise $40 million cash that it used to

release accused murderers, rapists, thieves and repeat criminals.[186]

- **Violence Lessened**: The violent protests in Minneapolis began to subside as the National Guard's presence increased to around 7,000.
- **Trump Praised Walz's Later Actions**: In a phone call with Walz and other governors, Trump complimented Walz for his response in the final days of the unrest, although this praise came after Walz's initial failures to contain the situation.[187]
- **Walz Urged More Protests**: Walz agreed with Trump that it was necessary to use force to put down the riots, but he argued that the next step was enabling peaceful protests to continue. He also said George Floyd's death "made us look at a reality that was always there, whether we didn't see it, or we didn't want to see it."[188]

June 3, 2020

- **Armed "Peace Officers"**: Black Lives Matter announced they would develop an armed branch of "peace officers" to combat police brutality.
- **Arrest of Other Police Officers**: Following intense public pressure and widespread protests demanding justice for George Floyd, Officers Thomas Lane, J. Alexander Kueng, and Tou Thao were arrested and charged with aiding and abetting second-degree murder and aiding and abetting second-degree manslaughter in connection with Floyd's death.

June 6, 2020

- **Defund the Police**: Black Lives Matter protestors began making the demand to Defund the Police, and on June 7, the Black Lives Matter official Twitter account posted a demand to Defund the Police.

June 17, 2020

- **Harris Encouraged Continued Protests**: Kamala Harris said in an interview that the protests were not going to stop, and they should not stop.[189]

Summer 2020-2021

- **Continued Damage and Looting**: Looting and damage to businesses continued well beyond the initial wave of riots. Businesses along Lake Street and University Avenue in St. Paul saw significant destruction, with some buildings being set on fire and others repeated looted. The state's emergency operations center demobilized on June 7, 2020 as rioting **subsided**, however, civil unrest and demonstrations persisted throughout 2020 and into 2021.
- **Occupation Continues**: The area known as George Floyd Square spanned several city blocks and was occupied from May 26, 2020 until well into 2023 by Black Lives Matter. The square was surrounded by barriers and checkpoints, and saw a sharp rise in crime, including shootings and drug activity, with local businesses suffering due to the lack of police

presence. Efforts by city officials to reclaim the space were met with resistance. The occupation raised serious concerns about lawlessness, economic impact, and the effectiveness of such prolonged anarchy in achieving meaningful reform.

- **Michael Freeman Protests**: Starting on May 27, 2020 and continuing into late 2020, Black Lives Matter organized protests outside the home of Hennepin County Attorney Michael Freeman for handling the initial prosecution of the officers too slowly.[190] Using lynch mob style intimidation tactics, they pressured him for quicker so-called justice by harassing his family, vandalizing his home and neighboring buildings, and leaving the neighborhood in a state of fear.
- **Damage to Police Precincts**: Even after June 1, areas near the Third and Fifth Police Precincts continued to see sporadic unrest, with buildings being targeted for vandalism and arson.
- **Opposition to Policing**: City Council members and Democrat Party leaders made statements including:
  - Lisa Bender, "Our commitment is to end our city's toxic relationship with the Minneapolis police department. To end policing as we know it."
  - Jeremiah Ellison, "This council is going to dismantle this police department."
  - Shivanthi Sathanandan, "We are going to dismantle the Minneapolis Police Department. Say it with me. DISMANTLE—the—Minneapolis—Police—Department." Sathanandan was

later violently carjacked in 2023 and called for tougher juvenile penalties.

August 1, 2020

- **Body Cam Videos**: The body cam videos from the four officers were finally released 70 days after George Floyd's death, showing Floyd resisting arrest, the drugs in his mouth, his claims that he couldn't breathe long before the Maximal Restraint Technique was used, and his attempts to kick the officers which lead to further restraint.

March 12, 2021

- **Settlement**: The family of George Floyd received $27 million from the city of Minneapolis in one of the largest pre-trial settlements in a civil rights wrongful death case in U.S. history.

April 20, 2021

- **Officer Chauvin Convicted**: Derek Chauvin, the officer who restrained Floyd with the Maximal Restraint Technique, was convicted of second-degree unintentional murder, third-degree murder, and second-degree manslaughter and sentenced to 22 years in prison.

February-June 2021

- **Other Officers Convicted**: The three other officers were found guilty in different proceedings of violating George Floyd's civil rights, aiding and abetting manslaughter and aiding and abetting second-degree murder, with each being sentenced to approximately three years of prison time.

REVIEW OF WALZ'S ACTIONS

Governor Walz has been heavily criticized for his handling of the Black Lives Matter Riots. Minnesota Congressman Walter Hudson summarized the governor's actions by saying, "Walz is a committed Marxist ideologue. This is obvious based on any exam of his record. When he was confronted with Minneapolis burning in the Floyd riots, his first response was to look for how to dismantle the institutions and disrupt the status quo. He didn't see the breakdown of law and order as a problem. In technology terms, he saw it as a feature not a bug.[191]

"Walz finally called in National Guard only under pressure, because he was going to be one-upped and embarrassed by Trump calling them in. His priority was upholding the Marxist ideology and keeping the Marxist faith and not protecting the business, neighborhoods, and people of Minnesota."[192]

Mayor Frey Blames Walz

Mayor Frey spoke out against Walz's handling of the riots, saying that Walz ignored repeated warnings about brewing violence in the city and rebuffed his requests to deploy the National Guard.[193]

Walz failed to act after Frey repeatedly raised the alarm about growing unrest in the city that led to widespread looting and the torching of a police precinct and hundreds of other buildings. Frey said he called Walz, a fellow Democrat, on the second night of unrest to warn him that a Target store was being looted and asked him to send in troops, but Walz was hesitant, saying he would consider it but didn't follow through for days.[194] "We expressed the seriousness of the situation. The urgency was clear," Frey said.

Frey insisted that he explicitly asked that night whether his verbal requests constituted a formal request for the National Guard, and the governor's staff confirmed that they did. But the governor's office pushed back on suggestions that it failed to quell rioting and said text messages and phone calls from Frey did not count as a formal request to send in the National Guard.

"I don't think the mayor knew what he was asking for," Walz has since said. "He wanted the National Guard, and what does that mean?" Walz said that he was following a process of waiting for Minneapolis leaders to formally request assistance before sending in the National Guard and that it was unprecedented to ask for assistance in a phone call. "We were staying in the lane that we were asked to support this," he said.

So, to be clear, Walz allowed for an unprecedented firing of four police officers by Mayor Frey without due process within hours of the death of someone they arrested, but Walz didn't allow for an unprecedented request for National Guard troops by phone and instead waited days before deploying the Guard.

Senate Blames Walz

Walz was accused by the Minnesota Senate's Joint Transportation and Judiciary and Public Safety Committee of downplaying the riots,[195] delaying the deployment of the National Guard and failing to coordinate with police. A report was developed from four joint committee hearings investigating the riots, recordings of press conferences, news articles, information requests (called "data practice requests" in Minnesota), and witness testimony. [196] The report concluded that the rioting, escalation of violence, and burning of the Third Police Precinct wouldn't have happened as quickly had government leaders acted faster.

Walz first mobilized the Minnesota National Guard 18 hours after Frey requested assistance, the report found. However, the Guard wasn't fully mobilized until four days after the first building was burned. "Him being so close and being a member of the National Guard, they should have been in as soon as the civil unrest, which they knew was going to happen," said State Senator Mark Koran.[197] "They should have been on call and should have been ready and raring to go. There should have been no hesitancy."

"For nearly a week at the end of May, Minnesotans watched in horror each night as Minneapolis descended further into chaos," Senate Majority Leader Paul Gazelka said. "They were begging for leadership that took far too long to arrive." "Above all else, this is a failure in leadership, and that leadership rests on Gov. Walz's shoulders. The governor cannot blame the mayors of Minneapolis and St. Paul." He said Walz should have called in the National Guard right away and thousands of Guard members should have been activated, instead of hundreds. Gazelka also said he believes there needed to be more proactive arrests of people committing crimes, and a curfew should have been in place by Thursday.

In response to Walz saying he was staying in his lane and waiting for someone to give him a plan before sending in the National Guard, Gazelka said Walz should not have been asking others for a plan."[198] "It was obvious that the Minneapolis mayor was in over his head. And I think that's where the governor needed to respond with emergency powers as commander-in-chief over our National Guard. The National Guard was simply waiting for a plan of action," Gazelka said.[199]

The report laid out four themes:

- Failure to Lead: Executive leadership at the state and local level failed to distinguish between demonstrators and rioters. Furthermore, leaders failed to provide the guidance Minnesotans expect from their offices.
- Philosophical Conflict Caused a Hesitation to Confront Ideological Allies: Walz and elected local leaders identified with the causes promoted by the demonstrators, causing them to lose sight of their responsibility to protect the public from criminal acts committed during the riots.
- Underestimation of the Escalation and Organization of the Riots: Walz did not realize the severity of events as they unfolded, resulting in a delayed reaction and increased violence.
- Refusal to Confront Criminal Violence with Force: Walz and Frey initially chose to negotiate with and appease the rioters rather than give law enforcement the authority to confront criminal acts with enough force to restore law and order. A primary responsibility of the Office of the Governor of the State of Minnesota and local elected officials is to protect the public. Inaction on the part of state and local officials led to an increase in violence.

The report gave several recommendations:

- Law enforcement at all levels of government must be given necessary equipment, personnel and authority to confront and stop riots before they escalate.
- Those who commit criminal acts under the guise of social protest must be arrested and prosecuted.
- Elected leaders in both the executive and legislative branches must recognize that public safety is a critical necessity.

It is surprising that anyone would need to point out that elected leaders must recognize that public safety is a critical necessity, but with Walz it was necessary.

Walz's Police Reforms

The report found that in six days of riots, the St. Paul Fire Department responded to over 1,150 calls.

Since the Black Lives Matter riots in 2020, Walz has signed at least twelve police reforms in bills or executive orders. Curiously, after the withholding of the body cam videos in the arrest and death of George Floyd for 70 days, Walz ordered expanded requirements for the use of body cameras during police interactions.

In May 2023, Walz signed a Public Safety Omnibus Bill to reform the police. This bill included a controversial law prohibiting the use of certain physical restraints by School Resource Officers (SROs), including holds that put pressure on a student's torso. Many police departments pulled their SROs from schools out of concern that the restrictions could limit their ability to effectively manage dangerous situations. Walz kept SROs out of schools for months while violence and disruption reached all-time highs.

As part of his push to include controversial books in children's library catalogues, Walz's administration has also pushed to use a book in 4th grade classes called *Something Happened in Our Town*. This children's picture book describes police as violent and racist and part of a pattern of racism. The Minnesota Police and Peace Officers Association sent Walz a letter saying they "learned that several departments in your administration are counseling teachers and parents to use materials which instill fear of police officers in young children... Our members deserve better from this state than to see their profession demonized. Their families deserve better from this state than to see their loved ones who risk their lives disparaged and unfairly cast as violent and racist, and we hope you agree[200]

After dramatic evidence of government abandonment and opposition to the police force, the number of police officers is decreasing. In May of 2020, there were 892 police officers serving in Minneapolis. As of October 2023, 380 officers have left, leaving the city with just over half of the officers it previously had. The overall number of police officers in Minnesota has decreased as well.[201]

Walz's actions are in keeping with Marxist ideology, which is inherently against institutions like the police that are viewed as tools of the ruling capitalist class to maintain control and suppress the working class. Marxists believe that in a classless and stateless society, the traditional functions of the police would theoretically become obsolete because the need for a repressive police force would diminish, as social order would be maintained through communal cooperation rather than coercion. While this ideal is a fantasy, as evidenced in the violence and crime in the unpoliced George Floyd Square, Walz did succeed in the Marxist goals of dismantling at least part of the police through demoralization and giving up at least part of the territory he governed to mob rule.

Crime Rates Under Walz

As the police force in Minneapolis decreased and mob rule increased, crime rates went up by 200–500% in the years following the riots.

Minneapolis[202]

	Carjackings	Gunshot Wounds	Homicides
2019	101	266	48
2020	388	551	84
2021	655	658	93
2022	542	544	81

Similarly, crime skyrocketed throughout Minnesota after Walz allowed violent criminals to go undeterred in the George Floyd Riots.

Minnesota[203]

	Aggravated Assault	Arson	Murder
2019	6,742	462	117
2020	8,203	710	185
2021	10,967	716	201
2022	10,342	828	182

Both Tim Walz and Jocob Frey have talked about violent crime going down in their state and city.[204] But the small downtick in violent crime is just a fraction toward what crime rates before they encouraged racist narratives, allowed undeterred looting, arson and violence, encouraged ongoing protests, ceded control of a section of a city to violent Black Lives Matter protestors, and demoralized the police.

It appears that Walz does not want violent criminals to be behind bars. He does not want Black Lives Matter rioters to be arrested. He does not want sex traffickers to be interfered with, or impregnate girls and force them into abortion. He does not even want illegal immigrants to be detained. The only crimes Walz seems to care about are those he deems hate crimes (in which he serves as the judge, jury and executioner) and those that involve breaking COVID regulations for non-riot related reasons.

Costs to Citizens

The costs of allowing such widespread destruction and devastation were high for the taxpayers of Minnesota. When Walz entered office, Minnesota had a $1.5 billion budget surplus. After passing the larges budget in Minnesota history, and making up for the costs from the riots, Minnesota now has $7.8 billion in outstanding debt.[205]

A Minnesota Senate report estimated that $500 million in property damage was done in the Twin Cities after the death of George Floyd, including more than 1,500 businesses and buildings that were burned.[206] There also were more than 160 fires. The city estimates it will cost $10 million to restore the Third Precinct which was abandoned to rioters and torched, and which has not been rebuilt to this day.[207] Taxpayers spent nearly $13 million to deploy about 7,000 National Guard members to clear the rioters.[208] And $27 million was given to the family of George Floyd in a civil settlement.[209] Overall, the riots cost Minnesota taxpayers more than half a billion dollars.

The riots also worsened the financial struggles for small businesses that were already hit hard by Walz's COVID-19 lockdowns. In cities like Minneapolis, many businesses, particularly those owned by minorities, were looted or burned down during the riots, compounding the economic devastation caused by the pandemic. Many small business owners were already struggling to survive under Walz's COVID restrictions and were then faced with rebuilding in the wake of the riots (Evrim Ağacı).

Walz has since tried to get money from other states' taxpayers to cover the costs of these choices. In July 2020 he asked President Trump for $500 million and to declare a "major disaster" in a request to the Federal Emergency Management Agency because of extensive damage to public infrastructure in the riots. He also asked the Federal Emergency Management Agency (FEMA) for $16 million to help cover the costs of cleanup, repairs, and infrastructure rebuilding from the extensive damage. Both of these requests were denied, leaving Minnesota to rely on state resources and private donations for recovery efforts. In addition, Walz asked for federal help by requesting a U.S. Small Business Administration (SBA) disaster declaration that would allow low-interest loans to help property owners rebuild. His request was granted, providing SBA loans to assist in covering uninsured losses and helping restore damaged property to its pre-disaster condition.

WRAP UP

The philosophy of Tim Walz which appears to align itself with Marxist ideology and groups like Black Lives Matter seemed to make him hesitate to stop the riots in his state. His words included racially charged narratives and virtue signaling that had the potential to inflame a crowd even further to violence and destruction. And the outcome of the riots appeared to accomplish Marxist goals of decreasing the presence and effectiveness of the police in his state.

As the country increasingly understands what woke means, the attempt to take over our nation's institutions by BLM and DEI enforcers like Kamala Harris and Tim Walz will only get more frantic. If wokeism did this to Minneapolis, image what it could do if unleashed in a similar way nationwide. In addition, we're left to question Tim Walz's recent attendance of a segregated all white, all male meeting of White Dudes for Kamala and ask if his racial narratives are just posturing and a means to an end.

Overall, Walz's COVID lockdown orders, combined with the George Floyd riots created a pincer move targeting the productive, the virtuous and the innocent of Minnesota. If you weren't a violent rioter, your life was made very difficult. You couldn't run your business, send your kids to school, or say goodbye to a dying loved one. You were locked down under some of the most aggressive orders in the nation. But if you were an arsonist, you could run around in street setting businesses on fire without fear of anyone stopping you. In so many ways, Walz's decisions encouraged the actions of the guilty and left the innocent holding the bag.

CHAPTER 8

China and Marxism—Little Bad Mouth

"One man's socialism is another man's neighborliness."

—Tim Walz

Why does Tim Walz take the far-Left positions he does on the sexualization of children, abortion, COVID, race riots, and more, and how did his time in the Army National Guard play a role in this? It all has to do with his connections to China, and the man he would become as he absorbed the doctrines of socialism.

WALZ'S CONNECTIONS TO CHINA

Tim Walz spent considerable time in China and praised it over and over. He arrived in the country, according to the students he taught, "speaking zero Chinese," but learned to speak both Mandarin and Cantonese during his time there. From his own accounts, he fell in love with the country, and it became a central part of his life as he lived and worked and traveled there more than 30 times.

Teaching a Chinese Communist Party-Approved Course

In the 1989-1990 school year, during a period of extreme political repression, Walz made his first trip to China. Walz was a high school teacher and a member of the Army National Guard. Although Walz has claimed he was there because he was offered an opportunity by Harvard University to gain a new perspective on global education through teaching in China, as so often is true with his statements about his military service and other professional endeavors, this claim has been inflated. He was actually volunteering at a high school in China under the auspices of World Teach,[210] a nonprofit program started by former Harvard University students. This organization also partners with Changsha Yuanjing Education Consulting Limited, a company affiliated with China's Ministry of Public Security, according to public records.[211]

For ten months he stayed, teaching a program sanctioned by the Chinese Communist Party (CCP) while the Chinese government brutally suppressed pro-democracy protests. During this trip, while Walz was visiting Hong Kong,[212] the Tiananmen Square protests began in April and ended on June 4 when the communist government massacred the protestors. [213] The Chinese Red Cross initially estimated the death toll at around 2,000, but this number was later retracted due to the Chinese government's strict control over information and their suppression of independent reporting. After the massacre, Walz took a train to Beijing to visit the square, recalling that there were many people at the train station who were "very angry that we would still go after what had happened."[214]

Walz's course of American culture and English as a second language, taught to 1,000 high school and middle-school students each week, was part of a broader CCP initiative to promote its ideological narrative during this time of severe repression.[215] So while his topic was American culture, his teachings were CCP-sanctioned content that aligned with the Party's thinking at the time of the massacre.

Upon returning to the United States, Walz told local newspapers how much he enjoyed his time in China.[216] "No matter how long I live, I will never be treated that well again," he recalled in 1990. "They gave me more gifts than I could bring home. It was an excellent experience."[217] An interview of one of his former colleagues in the Chinese-language outlet Initium Media noted that Walz had been treated "like royalty" while he was there.[218]

While Walz's strong praise for China underscored his detachment from the regime's human rights abuses and authoritarian practices, it wasn't a wonder that they treated him so well. The Chinese Communist Party would have had good reason to try to recruit and exploit a foreign military serviceman like Walz.

Honeymoon in China

After his first trip to China in 1989, Walz returned to his teaching job in America and hung a "Chinese banner" in his school office.[219] On June 4, 1994, Walz married Gwen Whipple. His wife revealed that he intentionally chose their wedding date to coincide with the fifth anniversary of the Tiananmen Square massacre of 1989. "He wanted to have a date he'll always remember," said Gwen Walz.[220]

The couple spent their honeymoon in China, along with sixty students[221] they brought with them, visiting Tiananmen Square on their trip and kicking off the first of many student exchange trips to the communist country.

Walz's choice to visit Tiananmen Square on such a significant date, combined with his favorable comments about China, suggests an alignment with the Chinese regime and its violent crackdown on pro-democracy protesters. In addition, people tend to honeymoon in places that resonate with them ideologically. Similarly, Bernie Sanders, who positions himself as a socialist, honeymooned in Russia.[222]

Cultural Exchange Programs

For decades following his first visit, Tim Walz traveled to and from China.[223] After this first trip, Walz and his wife founded the company called Educational Travel Adventures to send American kids to learn and study and experience China, the country he loved so much.[224] This student exchange program was subsidized by the CCP to bring students to China for the purposes of spreading the good news about communism[225]. Shockingly, Chinese authorities reportedly covered "a large part of the cost" of the first summer trip.[226] The next year, Walz and the Chinese government jointly sponsored scholarships for American students to visit China. Between 1989 and 2003, Walz travelled with hundreds of students to China.[227]

According to press accounts in local Midwestern papers, Walz told American students who were participating in this cultural exchange to downplay their Americanness. That could possibly seem like an innocuous comment if someone were thinking about how much energy and spirit Americans have, but as a cultural exchange it's certain Walz would never have told Chinese students coming to the U.S. to play down their Chineseness. Students also say Walz said things like, "In China, nobody is poor because everybody shares in China, as if the compulsive arm of the CCP is voluntary.[228]

One former student on a 1995 trip said he was struck by Walz's adoration for China and its communist ideology. "There was no doubt he was a true believer. At night, we'd go out, we'd walk the street fairs. We'd be buying souvenirs, and Tim was always buying the little red book. He said he gave them as gifts. I saw him buy at least a dozen on the trip."[229] This would be similar to being in Germany and buying copies of Mein Kampf to hand out to friends and family.

Walz traveled to China annually from 1996 until at least 2003. His travels were not merely for tourism; he was also granted a special work visa by the Chinese government.[230] Walz has claimed to have taken more than 30 trips to China during these years, and some took place while he was a senior ranking member of his state's Army National Guard.[231]

Chinese Communist Party Sanctioned University

In addition to teaching high school in China and traveling there dozens of times with hundreds of students, Walz also lectured at a Chinese state-run university.[232] Walz was a visiting fellow at the CCP-sanctioned Macau Polytechnic University until at least 2007, according to public filings and press reports. Macau was a former Portuguese colony, taken over by China. The school was established in 1981 and subscribes to the vision of China's Belt and Road Initiative—a massive infrastructure program that is the cornerstone of Chinese leader Xi Jinping's aggressive pursuit of influence overseas. Walz lectured there on international relations.

Comparison of America to China

While Walz has repeatedly praised China and his many times there, he has compared America to the communist country in the least favorable light possible. In various statements, Walz has drawn parallels between the violent suppression of pro-democracy protesters in China in 1989 and the historical injustices faced by Native Americans at Wounded Knee one hundred years before.[233] In so doing, he has tried to create a moral equivalence between the two.

The Wounded Knee massacre, which occurred in 1890, involved the killing of hundreds of Lakota Sioux by U.S. soldiers during the westward expansion. On the other hand, the Tiananmen Square massacre was a state-sanctioned murder by the Chinese government of thousands of civilians advocating for political freedom and democratic reforms.[234]

When the killing at Wounded Knee took place and the word spread, the consensus quickly became that it was a terrible scar on American history. In comparison, the official stance of the Chinese government is to minimize the scale of the events that happened at Tiananmen Square.[235] The wife of China's President Gee was a very famous singer at the time, and she even serenaded the troops following the massacre.[236] So while Walz attempted to drag America down to China's lowest level in what seems like an attempt at making excuses for China's conduct, his comparison failed to acknowledge how the two countries dealt with the marks on their records.

CCP Leaders at Walz's Inauguration

In January 2019, Walz invited a CCP diplomat and other CCP government officials to attend his gubernatorial inauguration. According to the translated Chinese government press release, "Acting Consul General Liu congratulated Governor Waltz and expressed his expectation to strengthen cooperation with the new Minnesota government to jointly promote the friendly and cooperative relations between Minnesota and China."[237] The CCP Diplomat left the Walz inauguration to meet with Walz cronies at Minnesota's premier globalist non-governmental organization (NGO), Minnesota Global.[238]

Secret Chinese Police Stations

Over 100 secret Chinese police service stations are operating across 53 countries, according to the Safeguard Defenders, a Spanish-based human rights group.[239] Seven of these stations are in the U.S., with one in Minnesota. These so-called "Overseas Chinese Service Centers" (OCSCs) are operated by the Chinese Communist Party's (CCP) United Front Work Department (UFWD), which has been characterized by the U.S.-China Economic and Security Review Commission as a "Chinese intelligence service."[240] Housed within various U.S.-based nonprofits, the OCSCs were ostensibly set up to promote Chinese culture and assist Chinese citizens living abroad, according to Chinese government records.[241]

However, Chinese nationals who run these police stations embed themselves in US cities to operate an "illegal overseas police station," according to counterterrorism experts.[242] The police stations "cooperate with Chinese intelligence" in order to "intimidate Chinese that are living in the United States that don't like the CCP or [are] critical of the CCP."[243] And there have been at least half a dozen documented cases where these networks have abducted Chinese people living in the United States, and sent them back to mainland China.[244]

The St. Paul branch secret CCP police outpost is housed by the Chinese American Association of Minnesota (CAAM) according to reports,[245] which is part of a global network of institutions overseen by the Chinese government.[246] In 2022, CAAM partnered with the group Minnesota Global to send delegations to China.[247] Walz helped establish Minnesota Global by defining its mission and objectives, securing early support, and using his political network to connect the organization with key stakeholders and decision-makers. Walz even participated in trade missions and events organized by Minnesota Global. His participation helped elevate the organization's profile and facilitated valuable connections.[248] And Walz has a long history of attending events organized by CAAM members, including one 2022 fundraiser for his gubernatorial campaign. [249]

Since the riots of 2020, Walz has talked ad nauseam about abuses by the local Minneapolis police, and their terrible behavior with regards to how they arrest people. But not once has he made any known criticisms of the Chinese secret police station in his state. People are left to wonder why Walz is so critical of his own country, but not China and why he hasn't called out the Chinese secret police on harassing people who live in his state.

A "Complicated Relationship"

Walz and his supporters would like people to believe that his cozy ties to the Chinese Communist Party (CCP) are not unusual. In fact, he is a "hawkish"[250] and staunch critic of the CCP's human rights abuses, his media allies say.[251] The liberal mainstream media uses messaging tactics such as saying Walz's relationship with China defies easy stereotypes,[252] is nuanced,[253] and can't be put in a box.[254] And Walz himself says of his Chinese obsession that he is "neither a 'dragon slayer' nor a 'panda hugger.'"[255]

A Walz spokesperson told the media: "Throughout his career, Governor Walz has stood up to the CCP, fought for human rights and democracy, and always put American jobs and manufacturing first...Vice President Harris and Governor Walz will ensure we win the competition with China, and will always stand up for our values and interests in the face of China's threats."[256]

The Chinese, however, have an expression for what Walz has done. It's called "big help with a little bad mouth."[257] And it's the practice of providing cover for the communist regime while issuing the occasional muted critique. Walz has talked about the human rights condition in China, but never in the context of doing anything about it.[258]

In 2016 Walz went to China with a few other Democrats and met with Premier Li. During this meeting, he told the Premier that he shouldn't look to the United States as an example of how to do human rights, because we don't know how to do it right either. He created a moral equivalence that the Chinese system is not any worse than America's, which is exactly what China wants from the United States. And that is exactly what Walz has done over the years—talk about human rights, but don't do anything about it.[259]

After all, if Walz were a sincere critic of China's human rights abuses, why would they have approved the courses he taught? Why would the CCP subsidize his trips to bring students to their country? The secret Chinese police harass and abduct people who speak openly against the CCP, so if Walz were sincerely speaking out against their atrocities, why would CCP members attend his inauguration as governor and why would Chinese diplomats congratulate him? The answer is they wouldn't do these things if he didn't share their ideology.

MARXIST IDEOLOGY

Marxism is the belief that there is the imbalance of power between capitalists and workers in industrial societies. The solution to that imbalance is revolution. The revolution overthrows the capitalist class and ushers in a new classless and stateless socialist society where order is maintained through communal cooperation rather than coercion.

However, regimes in the Soviet Union, China, Cambodia, and Cuba underwent Marxist-style revolutions, and these socialist/communist governments racked up a body count of nearly 100 million of their own people. They are remembered for their gulags, show trials, executions, and mass starvations. In practice, Marx's ideas unleashed man's darkest brutalities.

By the mid-1960s, Marxist intellectuals in the West realized that workers' revolutions would never occur in Western Europe or the United States, where there were large middle classes and rapidly improving standards of living. But rather than abandon their Leftist political project, they simply adapted their revolutionary theory to the social and racial unrest of the 1960s. Abandoning Marx's economic dialectic of capitalists and workers, they substituted race for class and sought to create a revolutionary coalition of the dispossessed based on racial and ethnic categories. For this reason, critical race theory is the representation of Marxism in the U.S., while communism is the political apparatus for accomplishing Marxism in places like China, and socialism is a term for a light version of political communism.

Walz's leftward bent finds its foundation in Marxism. His emphasis on race relations, revolution and a classless society shows the western influence on his ideology. On the other hand, his obsession with China and their communist regime gives his particular application of Marxism its Maoist flavor.

Marxist Ideologies

Walz's Marxist ideology permeates his words and actions, and can be seen in many if not all of his public policies.

- **Sexualization of Children**—In Marxism traditional family structures and sexual norms are tied to the development of private property and class society.[260] Communist thinkers have advocated for the abolition of traditional family structures and the normalization of diverse sexual practices, believing that communism would lead to the emancipation of sexual relations and communal living, and the dissolution of private property would enable more fluid and egalitarian sexual relationships.[261] Walz's promotion of sexual liberty, especially to the young generation, sets a foundation for a Marxist society.
- **Abortion**—Marxism typically views abortion through the lens of increasing the workforce and equality for women. "Reproductive justice" is a popular pro-abortion message that boils down at its essence to God not being just because he made women to carry babies, and abortion being needed to correct this injustice and ensure sexual liberty without women being taken out of the workforce. In addition, communist regimes also use abortion and forced abortion as a tool for population control, which is in keeping with their ideal of central planning on population size to achieve economic and social objectives. Walz's promotion of abortion at all cost sets a stage for both a robust socialist workforce and the control of that workforce by the state.
- **COVID**—The measures used in Walz's COVID lockdowns were in keeping with the Marxist playbook. "The snitch hotline in Minnesota is straight out of CCP. Tim Walz is a very bright guy. None of this by

accident," said his former student who went with him to China.[262] So too are the indefinitely extended emergency powers and the almost endless executive orders he issued. Marxist ideals promote a "dictatorship of the proletariat" as a transitional state in which the working class holds political power to dismantle the bourgeois state and suppress resistance from the former ruling classes in the transition to a classless society.[263] Unfortunately, as seen with Walz, this "temporary" transition turns indefinite as the new dictator resists giving up power.

- **Riots**—Walz repeatedly praised the riots in Minneapolis, indicating his heart and solidarity was with the rioters. He thought it was a pretty normal response, and he wanted the protests to continue after the National Guard was sent in. In addition, he delayed sending in the National Guard until more than a thousand buildings had been burned. As Minnesota Representative Walter Hudson stated, "His priority was upholding the Marxist ideology and keeping the Marxist faith; he didn't see the breakdown of law and order as a problem. In technology terms, he saw it as a feature not a bug."

Marxism views social and political unrest as a natural outcome of class struggle. Riots and uprisings are seen as manifestations of this underlying class conflict,[264] indicating that society is approaching a revolutionary moment and mobilizing against the ruling class.[265] In Marxist theory, such unrest can help to mobilize and radicalize the working class and become a catalyst for overthrowing the existing capi-

> talist system and establishing a socialist state.[266] And in America, where critical race theory has been overlayed onto Marxism, Walz's encouragement of the riots in Minneapolis provided a perfect scenario of this struggle to play out.

"If there was any doubt about what I'm saying," claimed Walz's student, "just look at the policies enacted by his administration, like the country's worst abortion law, anti-free speech, the riots. He's a Maoist to the core and should not be underestimated."[267]

Marxist Propaganda

A video on YouTube shows four straight minutes of Vice President Harris repeating the phrase, "I can imagine what can be, unburdened by what has been."[268] With her many verbal gaffs and anxious laughter, audiences have asked if this saying is just another example of her speaking word salad. But this statement is in fact a Marxist incantation, which may explain why she repeats it like it's a spell. The goal is to see the possibility of a world that is unburdened from its own history.

This is what Mao Zedong, the founder of the People's Republic of China did when he launched the campaign to destroy the "Four Olds" in 1966.[269] The Old Things were described poisoning the minds of the people for thousands of years, and fostered by exploiting classes.[270] But which customs, cultures, habits, and ideas specifically constituted the "Four Olds" were never clearly defined.[6] Calls to destroy the "Four Olds" were usually contrasted with the hope of building the "Four News," which also went undefined. [6]

The Bolsheviks pursued the same thing when they took power over Russia. They sought to make the new Russia or a socialist utopia, with a "new man" that was transformed in nature to embody the values and ideals of the new socialist society.[271] They implemented extensive educational and propaganda emphasizing Marxist ideology, with a focus on developing the new socialist consciousness among the youth. This included promoting collective over individualistic values, emphasizing the importance of the working class, and encouraging loyalty to the state.[272]

Vice President Harris, as the second in command of the greatest nation on Earth, and the daughter of a Marxist professor father, appears to have the knowledge to understand the propaganda she is repeating. Similarly, Tim Walz has demonstrated throughout his time as governor the desire to unmake what has been, and make it over according to Marxist ideals.

In addition to this messaging strategy, another message that has risen to the surface in the Harris/Walz campaign is the idea of the politics of joy. This message took root after the message of "saving the democracy" backfired when the democratic process was circumvented to install Harris as the Democratic candidate. The campaign pivoted to a message of calling their opponents "weird," then seemed to settle on the politics of joy. Harris and the liberal media repeatedly call her a "joyful warrior,"[273] with Walz saying things like, "It took Kamala Harris to come onto the scene to tell us this is a joyful thing we're doing."[274] Perhaps this is a strategy to cover for her anxious laughter when she speaks, or perhaps it's additional propaganda promoting Marxism.

From a Marxist viewpoint, the "politics of joy" is a byproduct of achieving social justice and equality. For Marxists, true happiness is expected to come from a classless society that overcomes a capitalist system.[275] Joy and fulfillment are achieved, according to Marxists, once the capitalist system is abolished and a socialist or communist society is established, leading to collective well-being.[276] Communal Happiness occurs, by Marxist definition, when everything is shared, from living spaces to sexual partners to children.[277] And State-Sponsored Happiness is the Marxist attempt to create joy through state-sponsored initiatives aimed at reinforcing communist ideals.[278]

The similarity between the propaganda materials used by Mao and other Marxist leaders and the messaging of Kamala Harris and Tim Walz is striking.[279] It underscores further their mutual commitment to try to make over any society they lead into a new Marxist utopia.

Price Controls

An August 2024 article in The Washington Post titled, "When your opponent calls you 'communist,' maybe don't propose price controls?" addressed the economic schemes of the Harris/Walz campaign.[280] Kamala Harris has stated that in the first 100 days of her presidency she would implement the first ever price control on food and groceries, "setting clear rules of the road to make clear that big corporations can't unfairly exploit consumers to run up excessive corporate profits on food and groceries."[281] But the "clear rules" and what is determined as "excessive" aren't defined. In 2020, Harris co-sponsored legislation with Elizabeth Warren to ban any "grossly excessive price" during any "atypical disruption" of a market, but no definition was provided for these terms, either.[282] This would allow the Federal Trade Commission to enforce bans using any metric it deems appropriate.

Tim Walz has taken similar steps in his own state and talked about the importance of price controls. Walz used his extended emergency powers during COVID to issue three of his 130 executive orders on price controls. to address price gouging during emergencies. For instance, during the COVID-19 pandemic, Walz issued executive orders to prevent price gouging on essential goods such as hand sanitizers and masks. He also tasked the Minnesota Department of Commerce with setting up hotlines and online reporting systems for residents to file complaints against businesses whose prices they believed were too high. Walz's administration actively enforced these measures. Walz used the Department of Commerce to conduct investigations into reported cases, as well as local law enforcement agencies, spreading their resources even thinner. When companies were deemed in violation, those online and in-store retailers were charged fines and restitution payments to the state.

"It's hard to exaggerate how bad this policy is," according to The Washington Post. "It is, in all but name, a sweeping set of government-enforced price controls across every industry, The New York Times has come out and said that this could "lead to shortages and distort market dynamics, as evidenced by historical examples such as the gas shortages during the Nixon administration when price ceilings were imposed." They also stated that these price controls can "often result in reduced supply and black markets as producers are disincentivized from selling at lower prices," and they can lead to "prolonged shortages and reduced innovation."[283]

The prospect of Kamala Harris and Tim Walz enforcing price controls is not only a dangerous precedent, but mirrors failed policies of communist and socialist regimes where government interference in pricing has led to chronic shortages and a lack of market responsiveness.[284] But by adopting similar measures, Harris and Walz would grant the government an enormous amount of power over economic activities, which is in keeping with Marxist ideology. Marxism's view of central planning and state control sees price controls as a temporary measure during the transition from capitalism to socialism, addressing the inequities of capitalist systems and redistributing resources more equitably[285]. But the ultimate solution is a complete overhaul of the capitalist system and its replacement with a socialist economy where resources and production are controlled collectively.[286] What seems curious in these Marxist revolutions, though, is that the collective control always ends up being control by the State; so the workers overthrew one government, only to have it replaced by a government that has more power than the last. It begs the question then if the leaders of a Marxist movement really want collectivism, or if they are setting themselves up to be dictators.

Patent Seizures

In 2019 C-SPAN coverage of a Townhall in Iowa, then US Senator Kamala Harris was running for Democratic nomination for president. At that meeting she said that for companies that developed prescription medication that was supported by federal funding for research and development, if those companies failed to "play by our rules…I will snatch that patent, and we will take over. Yes, we can do that. We can do that. The question is if you have the will to do it. I have the will to do it."[287]

Harris was engaging a conversation about prescription drug prices claiming she could take away patterns from companies who don't "play by our rules." And while the government does provide funding for drug research and helps organizations obtain patents for all kinds of products, it is currently not legal for a patent to be taken away based on how much a company wants to charge consumers for their product. In 2023 an effort was made to rewrite the Bayh-Dole Act of 1980 to give the federal government the power to take a patent because of price. The Biden/Harris administration supported this change, but the draft was not accepted.

Where this does happen though is in China. The Chinese Communist Party has been involved in the forced transfer or appropriation of intellectual property, for instance forcing foreign companies operating in China to transfer technology as a condition for market access.[288] This is part of the Marxist ideology of State Control and Central Planning where the government exerts extensive control over industries and businesses to align them with broader ideological and economic goals.

The practice of "snatching" patents also aligns with the Marxist principle of redistribution of wealth and resources to achieve greater equity. Communist regimes typically employ authoritarian methods to enforce policies and control aspects of society like economic practices. The reasonable question is would a Harris/Walz administration seek to adopt these Marxist ideals and authoritarian practices to make the United States more like China.

CONGRESSIONAL INVESTIGATIONS

Given the preponderance of evidence of Tim Walz's connections with China, it was no surprise when House Oversight Committee Chairman James Comer launched an investigation into Walz's "longstanding connections to Chinese Communist Party (CCP) entities and officials" on January 25, 2024. In addition, Congressman Jim Banks of Indiana also wrote to the U.S. Department of Defense (DOD) in February 2024 to inquire if Walz had a security clearance during his visits to the communist regime. Walz possessed a "concerning affinity for China," Rep. Banks told the DOD. "Any individual traveling dozens of times to an adversary nation in a personal capacity while having access to classified information poses an obvious security risk." Banks is requesting that Austin hand over information about the precise number of trips Walz took to China, what level of security clearance he held and for how long, and whether he attended foreign intelligence briefings and complied with reporting requirements.[289]

For 24 years, Walz served in the National Guard; first with the Nebraska National Guard, then with the Minnesota National Guard. As such, many of Walz's trips to China occurred while he was an active member of the National Guard. John R. Schindler, a former senior intelligence analyst and counterintelligence officer with the National Security Agency (NSA), wrote of Walz's ties to China, saying, "It's certain that Walz was vetted by the Ministry of State Security, the regime's powerful secret police, because that's how China works. No American would be allowed to run academic exchanges for a couple of decades, on the CCP's dime, without MSS approval. It just wouldn't happen.[290] "Three decades ago, a young American with an affection for China, who was also a part-time member of the U.S. military, would have been a tempting recruiting target for Chinese intelligence," added Schindler.

U.S. Sen. Tom Cotton of Arkansas summed it up by saying Walz "owes the American people an explanation about his unusual, 35-year relationship with Communist China."[291]

WRAP UP

During Walz's 2016 trip to China and meeting with Premier Li and Chinese officials, he recounted a story about something he did in in China in December of 1989. The Chinese officials stopped him and said, no, it was February of 1990 when he did that.[292] That's how closely the CCP has been tracking Walz since he was a young man. They saw him as someone worthy of investing that kind of time and attention into.

Through the decades, the dozens of trips and countless relationships, Walz's philosophical attraction to the left-wing Marxist doctrine has grown and been apparent. He's become so steeped in Chinese Communist Party ideology and practices, that he's even developed the nickname, The Great Walz of China.[293]

During an interview on September 6, 2020, Walz made the comment, "One man's socialism is another man's neighborliness" in a discussion on his policies and political philosophy.[294] He clearly sees socialism as an ideal societal structure for friendly Midwesterners, as well as America at large. But Walz's policies have never answered the question of what is so neighborly about taking people's property and agency away.

Instead, Walz has said, "With the proper leadership, there are no limits to what they could accomplish."[295] It leaves one to wonder, if he found himself in the position of Vice President of the United States, would he see himself as the leadership needed to help the Chinese Communist Party accomplish its goals.

CONCLUSION

The conventional analysis in a presidential race is that a candidate picks a running mate who strengthens his or her weaknesses. If you're far liberal, you choose a moderate. If you need geography, you choose someone from a swing state. Kamala Harris could have chosen Governor Josh Shapiro, a more moderate Democrat from Pennsylvania. He could have brought her the votes of those on the less radical side of the Left spectrum, and potentially a heavily contested swing state. Harris even announced her pick for VP in Philadelphia, leading everyone to think it was an inevitable choice. But it wasn't. Instead she chose Tim Walz, who amplifies her weaknesses and doesn't bring her critical electoral votes.

Walz is exactly like Kamala, who was ranked left of Bernie Sanders. This was a ranking she took pride in at the time. But since the announcement of her candidacy, the liberal media coverage of her far-Left stance has been largely removed from websites. Like so many of her unsavory attributes, it has fallen into an Orwellian memory hole, which is why a book like this is needed. And while Harris is almost as far Left on every single issue as possible, Walz may be further.

The white-haired, jovial Midwesterner (who happens to be younger than Brad Pitt but looks like his grandfather) makes emotional gesticulations and positions his brand as a nice old man, but Tim Walz is not a bumbling idiot. He may be reduced in his rhetoric to calling his opponents weird and making off-color and sexually nasty jokes about his VP rival, but according to his neighboring governor, Kristi Noem, he's actually "a bully and he pushes mandates down on his people."[296]

Lisa Zara, who lost her business in Walz's COVID lockdowns said when Harris announced Walz as her running mate, "Kamala made a big mistake picking him as her VP. She thought she was getting some Podunk freaking farmer. She didn't."[297]

But the question stands, is that what Kamala thought she was getting? By all appearances, Harris chose her dream socialist partner in Tim Walz, despite his inability to balance out her areas of weakness or to bring a needed state. His dreaminess comes wrapped in his love for China, promotion of abortion, transing of kids, executive overreach, and promoting revolutions to make over a society in a Marxist image. The real question is why Vice President Harris and those who advise her would think they could win an election without winning over the hearts and minds of those in the middle, or anyone other than the far Left.

"I don't think what Minnesota is getting in terms of its governor is an accurate reflection of its culture," said Minnesota State Rep Hudson. "There is a huge and increasing divergence between policy outcomes and the values that people actually hold. As a public official, how do you have no fear of the electorate?"[298]

The answer lies in the election process. Intentional Institutional mechanisms have been put in place under Walz's administration and others like him to keep the culture and values of the people on the ground from being reflected in the public policy of the leaders. For instance, by all historical trends and conventional analysis, the 2022 election in Minnesota was expected to be red wave, but it wasn't. So what happened?

Minnesota now has a 45-day-long voting period. Over that month and a half, ballots sit in mailboxes like live ammunition. The goal is to collect as many as possible with your candidate's name on them and get them into ballot boxes. This could look like going door-to-door in targeted neighborhoods collecting from the people whose votes you want. It could look like offering a Starbucks gift card in exchange for a specific vote. It could even look like stealing ballots out of mailboxes or off printing house loading docks. And who is it that does those types of activities? Only the most committed fringe activists.

The changes in the voting process have fundamentally changed how an election works so that candidates with a charged group of radicals behind them don't have to worry about what people really want. They don't have to worry about being exposed for stealing valor and lying to the public about their military service. They don't have to worry about their track record of budget failures, extreme anti-child policies, or letting their cities burn. They just have to harvest more ballots than their opponent.

In this effort, Walz has signed a myriad of election bills expanding voting opportunities and reducing necessary voting requirements. While he has expressed support for voting without a driver's license, in his state, Walz addressed this issue by signing the "Driver's Licenses for All" bill, allowing noncitizens, including illegal immigrants to receive driver's licenses. An estimated 81,000 people are eligible to receive these licenses in Minnesota.[299] Less than two months later, Walz also signed the "Democracy for the People Act," permitting automatic voter registration through Driver and Vehicle Services (DVS).[300] In September of 2024, just two months before the presidential election, a noncitizen came forward to report having received a ballot in his mailbox. When asked, Walz's administration failed to explain how noncitizens made it onto Minnesota's voter rolls.[301]

Over the last two years in Minnesota, legislation is being crafted by special interests and fringe groups before it becomes a bill. There is a separation between the values of the jurisdiction and the governance outcomes they are seeing. And the reason for that is because the votes aren't reflecting the people. Walz's efforts have helped to change the election from an exercise in political persuasion, to an operational contest, where the only thing that's needed is to craft a better ground game to collect more ballots and get them in ballot boxes.[302] It doesn't matter where those ballots come from. There's no need to win hearts and minds. All that's needed is a radicalized group of people who understand the goal.

In Tim Walz, Kamala Harris chose for a running mate the person who is most like her. She chose an extreme radical despite the conventional wisdom that would call her to balance her own extremes. And she did this because they know they don't have to win the middle anymore; they can simply rely on the operational superiority of their party to make up the difference.

ENDNOTES

1 "5 Key Reasons That Kamala Harris Picked Tim Walz" - Katie Rogers – The New York Times – August 6, 2024 - https://web.archive.org/web/20240829211626/https://www.nytimes.com/2024/08/06/us/politics/harris-walz-vp-pick.html

2 Beretta 1301 Comp Pro Shotgun - https://www.beretta.com/en-us/product/1301-comp-pro-FA0003

3 https://www.reddit.com/r/springerspaniel/comments/1elshoe/minnesota_gov_tim_walz_out_in_the_field_pheasant/

4 "VIDEO: Tim Walz Attacks Rural Minnesota As 'Mostly Rocks and Cows'" - Republican Governors Association – November 2, 2017 - https://web.archive.org/web/20240824175656/https://www.rga.org/video-tim-walz-attacks-rural-minnesota-mostly-rocks-cows/

5 "Rocks and Cows of Minnesota" Facebook Page - https://www.facebook.com/rocksandcowsofminnesota/

6 "'Citizen soldier' Walz honed leadership in uniform" - Brian Bakst – MPR News – October 3, 2018 - https://web.archive.org/web/20240831032742/https://www.mprnews.org/story/2018/10/03/tim-walz-national-guard-career-minnesota-governor-race

7 "Serving with pride for 24 years" - Tim Walz - Winona Daily News - November 3, 2006 - https://www.newspapers.com/image/546269441/?clipping_id=152950896

8 "Tim Walz's military service record: What we can VERIFY" - Megan Loe – VeryifyThis.com - August 13, 2024 - https://webcache.googleusercontent.com/search?q=cache:https://www.

abc10.com/article/news/verify/elections-verify/tim-walz-national-guard-military-service-record-what-we-can-verify/536-6172c051-3cc6-4d1a-ae6f-ddc4b6c7cfb7

9 "Retired Pay" - United States Army - Document review date May 30, 2024 - https://web.archive.org/web/20240607062910/https://myarmybenefits.us.army.mil/Benefit-Library/Federal-Benefits/Retired-Pay?serv=127

10 "Minnesota National Guard officials weigh in on Walz service" - Matthew Medsger - The Lamar Ledger – August 14, 2024 - https://web.archive.org/web/20240815141033/https://www.lamarledger.com/2024/08/12/minnesota-national-guard-officials-weigh-in-on-walz-service/

11 "Gov. Walz's former National Guard command sergeant major describes timeline of Walz retiring" - CNN - August 9, 2024 - https://www.youtube.com/watch?v=Wj09nFnGKXg

12 Tim Walz's FEC Form 2 - Statement of Candidacy - February 10, 2005 - https://web.archive.org/web/20240901043606/https://docquery.fec.gov/pdf/112/25038731112/25038731112.pdf

13 "Walz Still Planning to Run for Congress Despite Possible Call to Duty in Iraq" - Press Release – Tim Walz for Congress – March 20, 2005 - https://web.archive.org/web/20050420004957/http://www.timwalz.org/pr.php?pr=1

14 "Minnesota National Guard officials weigh in on Walz service" - Matthew Medsger - The Lamar Ledger – August 14, 2024 - https://web.archive.org/web/20240815141033/https://www.lamarledger.com/2024/08/12/minnesota-national-guard-officials-weigh-in-on-walz-service/

15 "Guard united recognized for record deployment" - Sgt. Mary Flynn - National Guard Bureau - October 5, 2007 - https://web.archive.org/web/20240829183944/; https://www.nationalguard.mil/News/Article/573070/guard-unit-recognized-for-record-deployment/

16 NGB Form 22A: Correction to NGB Form 22 - September 10, 2005 - https://x.com/Mashman78748/status/1822002427828052410/photo/1

17 "Gov. Walz's former National Guard command sergeant major describes timeline of Walz retiring" - CNN - August 9, 2024 - https://www.youtube.com/watch?v=Wj09nFnGKXg

18 "J.D. Vance attacked Tim Walz on military record. His statement ignores the timeline" - Sara Swann - PolitiFact - August 9, 2024

- https://web.archive.org/web/20240826225019/https://www.PolitiFact.com/factchecks/2024/aug/09/jd-vance/jd-vance-attacked-tim-walz-on-military-record-his/

19 "Tim Walz on 'lies about my service record'" - Leigh Pomeroy - Twin Cities Daily Planet - November 3, 2006 - https://web.archive.org/web/20240826165622/https://www.tcdailyplanet.net/tim-walz-lies-about-my-service-record/

20 "Tulsi Gabbard is back from active duty after being cut off from her campaign" - Simone Pathé - Roll Call - August 29, 2019 - https://web.archive.org/web/20240420205829/https://rollcall.com/2019/08/29/tulsi-gabbard-is-back-from-active-duty-after-being-cut-off-from-her-campaign/

21 NGB Form 22A: Correction to NGB Form 22 - September 10, 2005 - https://x.com/Mashman78748/status/1822002427828052410/photo/1

22 "Paid letter: The Truth About Tim Walz" - Tom Behrends, Paul Herr - West Central Tribune - November 2, 2018 - https://web.archive.org/web/20240901012722/https://www.wctrib.com/community/letters/the-truth-about-tim-walz

23 The number of US presidents who served in combat roles varies depending on the definition of "combat role."

24 "Tim Walz's Military Service Deserves Scrutiny" - Editors - National Review - August 8, 2024 - https://web.archive.org/web/20240816040338/https://www.nationalreview.com/2024/08/tim-walzs-military-service-deserves-scrutiny/

25 "Politics and the English Language" - George Orwell - Horizon - April 1946 - https://web.archive.org/web/20240823212147/https://www.orwellfoundation.com/the-orwell-foundation/orwell/essays-and-other-works/politics-and-the-english-language/

26 Local Guard members to be activated in July – Brian Ojanpa – Mankato Free Press – June 18, 2003 - Link Unavailable

27 "Tim Walz's military service record: What we can VERIFY" - Megan Loe – VeryifyThis.com - August 13, 2024 - https://webcache.googleusercontent.com/search?q=cache:https://www.abc10.com/article/news/verify/elections-verify/tim-walz-national-guard-military-service-record-what-we-can-verify/536-6172c051-3cc6-4d1a-ae6f-ddc4b6c7cfb7

28 Minnesota in the Global War on Terrorism Post 9-11 Profiles - Page 374 - https://web.archive.org/web/20240829161210/https://www.lrl.mn.gov/docs/2023/mandated/231447.pdf

29 "True Lies: People Who Lie Via Telling Truth Viewed Harshly, Study Finds" - Press release - The American Psychological Association - 2016 - https://web.archive.org/web/20240228223606/https://www.apa.org/news/press/releases/2016/12/true-lies

30 "True Lies: People Who Lie Via Telling Truth Viewed Harshly, Study Finds" - Press release - The American Psychological Association - 2016 - https://web.archive.org/web/20240228223606/https://www.apa.org/news/press/releases/2016/12/true-lies

31 9/11 Day of Remembrance at the MN State Capitol (9/11/21) - https://youtu.be/2xXpYNWi1Jg?si=I2zL-yybZUORLaI3&t=5855

32 "Washington and Havana are stuck at a diplomatic impasse" - Eric Bazail-Eimil, Miles J. Herszenhorn - Politico – August 13, 2024 - https://web.archive.org/web/20240819113412/https://www.politico.com/newsletters/national-security-daily/2024/08/13/washington-and-havana-are-stuck-at-a-diplomatic-impasse-00173850

33 "COL War veterans enlist in political battles" - Courtney Mabeus – Rochester Post Bulletin - March 25, 2006 - https://webcache.googleusercontent.com/search?q=cache:https://www.postbulletin.com/news/col-war-veterans-enlist-in-political-battles

34 "Bush Chides Opponents Of His Iraq Plan" - James Klatell - CBS News - January 13, 2007 - https://web.archive.org/web/20180630000559/https://www.cbsnews.com/news/bush-chides-opponents-of-his-iraq-plan/

35 "Company, Left" - Joshua Green – The Atlantic – January/February 2006 Issue -https://web.archive.org/web/20240729162947/https://www.theatlantic.com/magazine/archive/2006/01/company-left/304529/

36 "Walz's Holy Trinity of Normal: Coach, Teacher, Veteran" - Joshua Green - Bloomberg -August 6, 2024 - https://webcache.googleusercontent.com/search?q=cache:https://www.bloomberg.com/news/newsletters/2024-08-06/tim-walz-vice-presidential-pick-stands-out-as-teacher-and-veteran

37 https://webcache.googleusercontent.com/search?q=cache:https://twitter.com/JoshuaGreen/status/1821266872832082117

38 Cached versions of page across multiple dates are unavailable, screen captures are available here: https://x.com/JordanSchachtel/status/1822007418751996249 - Permalink: https://webcache.googleusercontent.com/search?q=cache:https://x.com/JordanSchachtel/status/1822007418751996249

39 "Serving with pride for 24 years" - Tim Walz - Winona Daily News - November 3, 2006 - https://www.newspapers.com/image/546269441/?clipping_id=152950896
40 "Tim Walz Thanked Pelosi After She Recognized His Service 'On the Battlefield'" - Chuck Ross - The Washington Free Beacon - August 9, 2024 - https://web.archive.org/web/20240810042145/https://freebeacon.com/elections/tim-walz-thanked-pelosi-after-she-recognized-his-service-on-the-battlefield/
41 https://web.archive.org/web/20240811020706/https://www.defense.gov/About/Biographies/Biography/Article/643303/patrick-j-murphy/
42 https://x.com/KamalaHQ/status/1820918063966962143 - Permalink: https://webcache.googleusercontent.com/search?q=cache:https://x.com/KamalaHQ/status/1820918063966962143
43 "Walz 'misspoke' in saying he served 'in war,' Harris campaign says" - Aaron Pellish and Dana Bash – CNN – August 10, 2024 - https://web.archive.org/web/20240901025638/https://www.cnn.com/2024/08/10/politics/walz-national-guard-harris-campaign/index.html
44 "Minnesota National Guard officials weigh in on Walz service" - Matthew Medsger - The Lamar Ledger – August 14, 2024, https://web.archive.org/web/20240815141033/https://www.lamarledger.com/2024/08/12/minnesota-national-guard-officials-weigh-in-on-walz-service/
45 https://x.com/NoVA_Campaigns/status/1826469193350610988 - Permalink: https://webcache.googleusercontent.com/search?q=cache:https://x.com/NoVA_Campaigns/status/1826469193350610988
46 "Meet Governor Tim Walz" - Harris Walz Campaign - August 6, 2024 - https://web.archive.org/web/20240806143807/https://kamalaharris.com/meet-governor-tim-walz/
47 "Meet Governor Tim Walz" - Harris Walz Campaign - August 8, 2024 - https://web.archive.org/web/20240808130722/https://kamalaharris.com/meet-governor-tim-walz/
48 "Specialty coins are new Walz calling card" - Brian Bakst - MPR News - August 21, 2019 - https://www.mprnews.org/story/2019/08/21/specialty-coins-are-new-walz-calling-card
49 "US Army Ranks" - United States Army - https://web.archive.org/web/20240828192216/https://www.army.mil/ranks/

50 Army Regulations 600-8-19-7-1a - US Army - June 21, 2024 - https://www.moguard.ngb.mil/Portals/48/Documents/Human%20Resources%20PDFs/EPS/EPS%20Documents/AR%20600-8-19_21%20June%202024.pdf?ver=7QYfYwkgVXd-cvvGKidzlcg%3D%3D×tamp=1720461570677

51 "Minnesota National Guard confirms VP nominee Tim Walz demoted, calling into question official bio" - Steven Richards – Just the News – August 7, 2024 - https://web.archive.org/web/20240829162806/https://justthenews.com/politics-policy/past-criticisms-vp-nominee-tim-walzs-retirement-military-resurface

52 "Minnesota National Guard officials weigh in on Walz service" - Matthew Medsger - The Lamar Ledger – August 14, 2024, https://web.archive.org/web/20240815141033/https://www.lamarledger.com/2024/08/12/minnesota-national-guard-officials-weigh-in-on-walz-service/

53 https://apnews.com/article/tim-walz-drunken-driving-arrest-kamala-harris-b2ffe73963e0dbf9c804697e2831753e

54 https://leadstories.com/hoax-alert/2024/08/fact-check-tim-walz-did-coach-high-school-state-football-championship-team-did-not-lose-job-over-dui.html

55 https://x.com/amuse/status/1826596839719678138?lang=en

56 https://www.thedailybeast.com/cop-i-arrested-tim-walz-for-dui-why-did-his-aide-lie-about-it

57 https://www.thedailybeast.com/cop-i-arrested-tim-walz-for-dui-why-did-his-aide-lie-about-it

58 https://www.youtube.com/watch?v=avUKtmCb3wc

59 Cristine Trooien - Minnesota Parents Alliance

60 https://thehill.com/homenews/lgbtq/4808291-minnesota-governor-tim-walz-lgbtq-rights/

61 https://www.congress.gov/111/crec/2009/10/06/CREC-2009-10-06-pt1-PgH10505-2.pdf

62 https://www.mprnews.org/story/2023/06/26/photos-sun-shines-through-for-twin-cities-pride-parade

63 https://www.lrl.mn.gov/archive/execorders/21-25.pdf

64 https://www.youtube.com/watch?v=LZeEBKzturQ

65 https://knsiradio.com/2023/03/08/minnesota-governor-signs-gender-affirming-care-bill/; https://www.mprnews.org/story/2023/03/08/walz-moves-to-protect-those-seeking-gender-affirming-care

66 https://knsiradio.com/2023/03/08/minnesota-governor-signs-gender-affirming-care-bill/; https://www.mprnews.org/story/2023/03/08/walz-moves-to-protect-those-seeking-gender-affirming-care
67 https://x.com/MovingWorkSaint/status/1821570903169503570
68 https://www.pewresearch.org/short-reads/2024/03/25/what-the-data-says-about-abortion-in-the-us/#how-many-abortions-are-there-in-the-us-each-year
69 https://www.pop.org/many-american-women-felt-pressured-abortions-study-finds/
70 https://www.mprnews.org/story/2023/03/08/walz-moves-to-protect-those-seeking-genderaffirming-care
https://www.startribune.com/gov-tim-walz-signs-executive-order-protecting-gender-affirming-health-care/600257207
71 https://www.cbsnews.com/news/minnesota-abortion-law-tim-walz-governor-pro-act/
72 https://www.intomore.com/impact/politics/tim-walzs-gay-backstory-means-everything-to-queer-voters/
https://www.mprnews.org/story/2023/03/08/walz-moves-to-protect-those-seeking-genderaffirming-care
73 https://www.nationalreview.com/2008/08/dead-weight-editors/
74 https://ifstudies.org/blog/has-the-global-war-against-baby-girls-come-to-america
75 https://www.thenewatlantis.com/publications/the-global-war-against-baby-girls
76 https://thehill.com/homenews/lgbtq/4808291-minnesota-governor-tim-walz-lgbtq-rights/
77 https://www.frc.org/issueanalysis/us-abortion-law-in-comparison-with-the-globe; https://www.washingtonexaminer.com/opinion/op-eds/make-an-atrocity-determination-about-chinas-treatment-of-uighurs; https://www.bbc.com/news/world-asia-59144712; https://www.hrw.org/world-report/2019/country-chapters/vietnam; https://www.frc.org/get.cfm?i=PV21L02; https://www.washingtonpost.com/outlook/canada-is-heading-toward-a-human-rights-disaster-for-disabled-people/2021/02/19/01cbfca4-7232-11eb-85fa-e0ccb3660358_story.html
78 https://www.pewresearch.org/short-reads/2024/03/25/what-the-data-says-about-abortion-in-the-us/; https://eppc.org/publication/how-the-eugenics-movement-made-race-based-

abortions-normal/; https://19thnews.org/2024/08/tim-walz-views-abortion-education-lgbtq-guns-caregiving/; https://www.intomore.com/impact/politics/tim-walzs-gay-backstory-means-everything-to-queer-voters/; https://www.startribune.com/gov-tim-walz-signs-executive-order-protecting-gender-affirming-health-care/600257207

79 https://www.startribune.com/gov-tim-walz-signs-executive-order-protecting-gender-affirming-health-care/600257207

80 https://www.liveaction.org/news/dr-bernard-nathanson-ultrasound-abortion-pro-life/; https://abbyjohnson.org/; https://www.liveaction.org/what-we-do/abby-johnson/; https://www.silentnomoreawareness.org/testimonies/joyce-zounis.aspx; https://www.lifesitenews.com/news/doctor-who-performed-1200-abortions-testifies-before-congress-on-the-brutali/; https://www.silentnomoreawareness.org/testimonies/kathy-sparks.aspx

81 https://www.startribune.com/gov-tim-walz-signs-executive-order-protecting-gender-affirming-health-care/600257207

82 http://issuu.com/actionfund/docs/ppfa_financials_2010_122711_web_vf?mode=window&viewMode=doublePage

83 http://www.nationalrighttolifenews.org/news/2012/03/hhs-issues-new-rule-on-obamacare-scheme-to-fund-abortion-insurance/

84 https://www.pewresearch.org/short-reads/2024/03/25/what-the-data-says-about-abortion-in-the-us/; https://eppc.org/publication/how-the-eugenics-movement-made-race-based-abortions-normal/

85 https://www.startribune.com/gov-tim-walz-signs-executive-order-protecting-gender-affirming-health-care/600257207

86 https://www.pewresearch.org/short-reads/2024/03/25/what-the-data-says-about-abortion-in-the-us/; https://eppc.org/publication/how-the-eugenics-movement-made-race-based-abortions-normal/

87 https://www.mprnews.org/story/2023/03/08/walz-moves-to-protect-those-seeking-genderaffirming-care

88 https://www.intomore.com/impact/politics/tim-walzs-gay-backstory-means-everything-to-queer-voters/; https://www.mprnews.org/story/2023/03/08/walz-moves-to-protect-those-seeking-genderaffirming-care

89 https://mndaily.com/275193/uncategorized/walz-signs-abortion-rights-bill-into-law/; https://www.ap.org/news-highlights/

elections/2024/the-walz-record-abortion-rights-free-lunches-for-schoolkids-and-disputes-over-a-riot-response/

90 https://apnews.com/article/harris-abortion-minnesota-women-election-a4c4979fb71070daa1fde2038aa41f2b

91 https://communityhealth.mayoclinic.org/featured-stories/human-trafficking#:~:text=The%20majority%20of%20human%20trafficking,401%20sex%20trafficking%20victims%20identified

92 https://www.usnews.com/news/best-states/articles/2020-03-17/10-states-with-the-most-aggressive-response-to-coronavirus; https://blog.cheapism.com/coronavirus-restrictions/; https://www.beckershospitalreview.com/rankings-and-ratings/states-ranked-by-covid-19-restrictions.html; https://www.mprnews.org/story/2021/08/09/behind-the-scenes-walz-minnesota-covid-pandemic-response

93 https://www.startribune.com/what-you-need-to-know-about-minnesota-s-covid-19-restrictions/568484941

94 https://www.startribune.com/gov-tim-walz-to-sign-law-to-strengthen-abortion-rights-in-minnesota/600247932; https://www.mprnews.org/story/2023/01/31/walz-signs-bill-guaranteeing-abortion-access-in-minnesota

95 https://www.startribune.com/gov-tim-walz-to-sign-law-to-strengthen-abortion-rights-in-minnesota/600247932; https://www.mprnews.org/story/2023/01/31/walz-signs-bill-guaranteeing-abortion-access-in-minnesota; https://www.kare11.com/article/news/politics/appeals-court-minnesota-covid-peacetime-emergency-legal/89-dcfaeb9a-64ba-4c86-a751-045e610cde88; https://www.startribune.com/what-america-needs-to-know-about-tim-walz-of-minnesota/600386013

96 https://www.startribune.com/gov-tim-walz-to-sign-law-to-strengthen-abortion-rights-in-minnesota/600247932

97 https://www.mprnews.org/story/2023/01/31/walz-signs-bill-guaranteeing-abortion-access-in-minnesota

98 https://floridianpress.com/2024/08/desantis-launches-new-volley-of-walz-attacks-his-snitch-hotline-for-draconian-covid-laws/

99 https://floridapolitics.com/archives/688789-ron-desantis-snitch-walz/

100 https://tennesseestar.com/the-upper-midwest/one-minnesota-thousands-reported-on-neighbors-using-tattle-tale-hotline-during-pandemic/admin/2022/07/04/;

https://archive.is/o/dxgzX/https:/twitter.com/BirkMatt/status/1540066706437046272
101 https://archive.is/o/dxgzX/https:/mnbca.sharefile.com/share/view/s2b91a5fd6b424220b72b190179e29e5c/fo76057a-7407-4720-9bf6-1f2b14ea94a5
102 https://www.thebrownmanngroup.com/StolenValorImages
103 https://www.nytimes.com/2020/12/14/health/coronavirus-vaccine.html
104 https://www.fda.gov/news-events/press-announcements/fda-issues-emergency-use-authorization-pfizer-biontech-covid-19-vaccine
105 https://www.health.state.mn.us/diseases/coronavirus/vaccine/index.html; https://www.startribune.com/covid-19-vaccine-rolling-out-across-minnesota/573897191/; https://www.mprnews.org/story/2020/12/15/minnesota-begins-covid19-vaccine-distribution
106 https://www.mprnews.org/story/2021/10/26/walz-pawlenty-pair-up-again-to-get-promote-covid-shots
107 https://www.minnpost.com/wp-content/uploads/2021/10/2021_10_05_Legislative-Leaders-Special-Session.pdf; https://www.minnpost.com/state-government/2021/10/why-gov-tim-walz-couldnt-impose-a-vaccine-mandate-for-minnesota-even-if-he-still-had-emergency-powers/
108 https://www.cdc.gov/mmwr/volumes/72/wr/mm7218a4.htm
109 https://www.kare11.com/article/news/local/new-covid-vaccine-program-gives-minnesota-kids-200-gift-cards-scholarships/89-b4d0db2d-1418-4d75-8219-87dc9a164f9a
110 https://www.mprnews.org/story/2024/08/07/walz-education-track-record-minnesota; https://www.mprnews.org/story/2023/03/24/three-years-after-minnesotas-initial-covid19-shutdown-impacts-persist
111 https://www.politifact.com/article/2024/aug/21/fact-checking-tim-walz-before-his-2024-dnc-speech/
112 https://www.mprnews.org/story/2024/08/07/walz-education-track-record-minnesota; https://www.mprnews.org/story/2023/03/24/three-years-after-minnesotas-initial-covid19-shutdown-impacts-persist
113 https://www.mprnews.org/story/2023/03/24/three-years-after-minnesotas-initial-covid19-shutdown-impacts-persist

114 https://www.mprnews.org/story/2024/08/07/walz-education-track-record-minnesota; https://www.mprnews.org/story/2024/08/07/walz-education-track-record-minnesota

115 https://www.mprnews.org/story/2021/06/01/scofflaws-or-victims-businesses-that-broke-covid-rules-seek-amnesty; https://www.mprnews.org/story/2024/08/07/walz-education-track-record-minnesota

116 https://www.mprnews.org/story/2024/08/07/walz-education-track-record-minnesota

117 https://www.politifact.com/article/2024/aug/21/fact-checking-tim-walz-before-his-2024-dnc-speech/

118 https://www.mprnews.org/story/2024/08/07/walz-education-track-record-minnesota

119 https://www.startribune.com/gov-tim-walz-to-sign-law-to-strengthen-abortion-rights-in-minnesota/600247932

120 https://www.breitbart.com/politics/2024/08/11/former-minnesota-bar-owner-blasts-walz-evil-man-ripped-small-businesses-covid/

121 https://www.foxbusiness.com/economy/minnesota-sues-local-bar-after-it-opened-against-covid-19-restrictions; https://www.foxbusiness.com/media/ex-minnesota-bar-owners-say-evil-tim-walzs-far-left-policies-ruined-small-businesses; https://www.startribune.com/minnesota-small-business-owners-want-court-to-strike-down-gov-tim-walz-s-closure-orders/570056652

122 https://www.marshallindependent.com/news/local-news/2021/02/havens-garden-owner-says-fight-with-state-isnt-about-attention/; https://www.marshallindependent.com/news/local-news/2020/12/they-want-me-to-comply/

123 https://www.marshallindependent.com/news/local-news/2021/02/havens-garden-owner-says-fight-with-state-isnt-about-attention/; https://www.marshallindependent.com/news/local-news/2020/12/they-want-me-to-comply/

124 https://www.marshallindependent.com/news/local-news/2020/12/they-want-me-to-comply/

125 https://www.marshallindependent.com/news/local-news/2021/02/havens-garden-owner-says-fight-with-state-isnt-about-attention/; https://www.marshallindependent.com/news/local-news/2020/12/they-want-me-to-comply/

126 https://www.mprnews.org/story/2020/12/17/state-moves-to-enforce-walz-bar-order; https://www.mprnews.org/story/2020/12/17/state-moves-to-enforce-walz-bar-order
127 https://www.mprnews.org/story/2020/12/17/state-moves-to-enforce-walz-bar-order; https://www.startribune.com/minnesota-ag-sues-bars-that-defied-walz-ban-on-dine-in-service/573419111
128 https://www.startribune.com/minnesota-ag-sues-bars-that-defied-walz-ban-on-dine-in-service/573419111; https://www.startribune.com/minnesota-ag-sues-bars-that-defied-walz-ban-on-dine-in-service/573419111
129 https://www.foxbusiness.com/lifestyle/minnesota-businesses-plan-to-reopen-in-protest-of-covid-19-restrictions
130 https://www.foxbusiness.com/lifestyle/minnesota-businesses-plan-to-reopen-in-protest-of-covid-19-restrictions
131 https://www.startribune.com/minnesota-small-business-owners-want-court-to-strike-down-gov-tim-walz-s-closure-orders/570056652
132 https://www.foxbusiness.com/lifestyle/minnesota-businesses-plan-to-reopen-in-protest-of-covid-19-restrictions
133 https://www.foxbusiness.com/video/6360388973112
134 https://reason.com/2024/08/06/tim-walz-was-a-covid-19-tyrant/; https://www.aol.com/news/tim-walz-covid-19-tyrant-210456687.html
135 https://www.startribune.com/gov-tim-walz-to-sign-law-to-strengthen-abortion-rights-in-minnesota/600247932; https://www.mprnews.org/story/2023/01/31/walz-signs-bill-guaranteeing-abortion-access-in-minnesota
136 https://www.mprnews.org/story/2023/01/31/walz-signs-bill-guaranteeing-abortion-access-in-minnesota
137 https://www.startribune.com/court-hears-legal-challenge-to-minn-gov-walz-s-emergency-powers/571794782
138 https://www.startribune.com/unemployment-requests-spike-as-minnesota-businesses-close-for-covid-19/568877382/
139 https://www.startribune.com/in-lawsuit-minnesota-faith-groups-allege-church-business-closures-violate-constitution/570276802
140 https://www2.cbn.com/news/us/minnesota-finally-lifts-restrictions-worship-services-attorney-vows-justice-all-churches

141 https://www2.cbn.com/news/us/minnesota-finally-lifts-restrictions-worship-services-attorney-vows-justice-all-churches
142 https://www.startribune.com/gov-tim-walz-to-let-minnesota-churches-open-at-25-occupancy/570721802?refresh=true
143 https://www.mprnews.org/story/2021/01/06/new-year-new-covid19-regulations-in-mn-what-you-need-to-know
144 https://www.thefallofminneapolis.com
145 https://www.foxbusiness.com/media/ex-minnesota-bar-owners-say-evil-tim-walzs-far-left-policies-ruined-small-businesses
146 https://evrimagaci.org/tpg/tim-walzs-covid-policies-spark-outrage-among-business-owners-17872
147 https://www.startribune.com/court-hears-legal-challenge-to-minn-gov-walz-s-emergency-powers/571794782
148 George Floyd's rap collaborator remembers "legendary" freestyler" - Matthew Neale - NME.com - June 7, 2020 - https://www.nme.com/news/music/george-floyds-rap-collaborator-remembers-legendary-freestyler-2683242
149 Collin, L. (n.d.). *They're lying: The media, the left, and the death of George Floyd* (J. C. Chaix, Ed.).
150 https://www.nytimes.com/2020/05/31/us/george-floyd-investigation.html
151 https://wtf-usa.com/GeorgeFloyd_0793796_C.pdf
152 Harris County Court Records, Harris County, Texas
153 https://www.thefallofminneapolis.com
154 https://www.npr.org/2022/05/18/1099585400/george-floyd-biography-book
155 https://www.minnpost.com/metro/2020/05/what-we-know-about-the-events-surrounding-george-floyds-death-and-its-aftermath-a-timeline/#:~:text=Floyd%2C%20a%20resident%20of%20St,during%20the%20COVID%2D19%20pandemic.
156 Collin, L. (n.d.). *They're lying: The media, the left, and the death of George Floyd* (J. C. Chaix, Ed.).
157 https://www.thefallofminneapolis.com
158 https://www.youtube.com/watch?v=cFPi3EigjFA
159 https://www.washingtonpost.com/video/national/officer-lanes-bodycam-footage-from-george-floyds-arrest-released/2020/08/11/de80159a-e93d-44c0-9e02-54e7dd869e4b_video.html
160 https://www.minnpost.com/metro/2020/05/what-we-know-about-the-events-surrounding-george-floyds-death-and-its-af-

termath-a-timeline/#:~:text=Floyd%2C%20a%20resident%20of%20St,during%20the%20COVID%2D19%20pandemic.

161 https://www.oxygen.com/crime-news/medical-examiner-blames-police-pressure-for-george-floyds-death

162 https://www.startribune.com/defense-asks-medical-examiner-about-outside-pressures-during-george-floyd-death-investigation/600141363/; https://www.mprnews.org/story/2022/02/01/medical-examiner-who-ruled-floyds-death-a-homicide-takes-stand-in-3-ex-cops-trial

163 Collin, L. (n.d.). *They're lying: The media, the left, and the death of George Floyd* (J. C. Chaix, Ed.).

164 https://www.cnn.com/2020/06/01/us/george-floyd-independent-autopsy/index.html

165 https://people.com/crime/george-floyds-family-wants-1st-degree-murder-charge-says-independent-autopsy-shows-asphyxiation/

166 https://www.thefallofminneapolis.com

167 https://www.mprnews.org/story/2020/05/26/protesters-rally-to-call-for-justice-for-man-who-died-in-mpls-police-incident; https://www.cbsnews.com/minnesota/news/hundreds-of-protesters-march-in-minneapolis-after-george-floyds-deadly-encounter-with-police/

168 https://www.startribune.com/did-tim-walz-let-rioters-burn-down-minneapolis/601055269

169 https://www2.startribune.com/e-mails-public-records-reveal-what-happened-before-minneapolis-third-precinct-was-abandoned/566290701/

170 https://www.startribune.com/mpls-mayor-says-walz-hesitant-to-deploy-guard-during-riots/571999292/?refresh=true

171 https://web.archive.org/web/20220810002736/https:/lims.minneapolismn.gov/Download/RCAV2/26623/2020-Civil-Unrest-After-Action-Review-Report.pdf#page=21&zoom=auto,-73,789; https://www.startribune.com/mpls-mayor-says-walz-hesitant-to-deploy-guard-during-riots/571999292

172 https://web.archive.org/web/20220313005354/https:/www.lrl.mn.gov/docs/2020/other/200998.pdf#page=35&zoom=auto,-73,782

173 https://www.thefallofminneapolis.com

174 https://www.foxnews.com/politics/minneapolis-mayor-says-facemasks-given-to-rioters-as-other-residents-told-to-avoid-mass-gatherings

175 https://www.cnn.com/2020/07/01/politics/fact-check-trump-walz-minnesota-national-guard/index.html

176 https://lims.minneapolismn.gov/Download/FileV2/22031/Mayoral-Declaration-of-Local-Emergency.pdf

177 https://mn.gov/governor/assets/EO 20-64 Final_tcm1055-433855.pdf

178 https://x.com/GrageDustin/status/1823081138664988676

179 https://nypost.com/2024/08/07/us-news/gwen-walz-said-she-kept-windows-open-during-george-floyd-riots-to-smell-burning-tires/

180 https://www.startribune.com/mayor-frey-gov-walz-hesitated-to-deploy-national-guard-during-minneapolis-riots/571999292; https://twitter.com/MNNationalGuard/status/1266212998009536512

181 https://x.com/WhiteHouse45/status/1266342941649506304?s=20

182 https://nypost.com/2020/05/30/minnesota-gov-tim-walz-compares-george-floyd-riots-to-military-operation/

183 https://mn.gov/governor/assets/EO%2020-65%20Final_tcm1055-434635.pdf; https://www.fox9.com/news/fires-chaos-return-to-minneapolis-as-many-defy-curfew

184 https://www.cbsnews.com/news/tim-walz-minnesota-governor-fully-mobilizes-national-guard-first-time-in-history-george-floyd-death-protests/

185 https://x.com/KamalaHarris/status/1267555018128965643?lang=ena

186 https://nypost.com/2024/08/25/opinion/kamala-harris-support-for-bail-fund-that-freed-violent-criminals-shows-how-tough-on-crime-she-really-is/

187 https://abcnews.go.com/US/despite-new-criticism-trump-told-walz-2020-happy/story?id=112616502

188 https://www.cbsnews.com/news/audio-donald-trump-praised-tim-walz-handling-riots-george-floyd-death-2020/

189 https://www.youtube.com/watch?v=NTg1ynIPGls

190 https://www.startribune.com/

191 Personal interview with Rep. Walter Hudson

192 Personal interview with Rep. Walter Hudson

193 https://www.startribune.com/mpls-mayor-says-walz-hesitant-to-deploy-guard-during-riots/571999292/?refresh=true
194 https://nypost.com/2020/05/30/minnesota-activates-national-guard-troops-as-protests-continue/
195 https://nypost.com/2024/08/06/us-news/tim-walz-failed-to-act-as-blm-rioters-burned-minneapolis-in-2020-state-senate/
196 https://www.thecentersquare.com/minnesota/article_8739afc4-0d94-11eb-8437-97f5f97f865d.html
197 https://www.foxnews.com/politics/minnesota-lawmaker-sounds-alarm-gov-walzs-radical-agenda-election-heinous
198 https://www.startribune.com/gov-tim-walz-laments-abject-failure-of-riot-response/570864092
199 https://www.startribune.com/gov-tim-walz-laments-abject-failure-of-riot-response/570864092
200 https://www.facebook.com/MNPoliceAssn/posts/378936513462029
201 https://www.startribune.com/; https://www.mprnews.org/; https://www.minnpost.com/
202 https://www.minneapolismn.gov/government/government-data/datasource/crime-dashboard/
203 https://dps.mn.gov/divisions/ooc/news-releases/Pages/BCA-Releases-2022-Uniform-Crime-Report.aspx
204 https://www.startribune.com/violent-crime-drops-minnesota-minneapolis-twin-cities-metro-2023/601117582; https://www.startribune.com/minnesotas-violent-crime-went-down-in-2022-but-not-significantly-new-bca-report-finds/600303811
205 https://mn.gov/mmb-stat/documents/budget/operating-budget/forecast/feb-2024/feb24-dcf.pdf
206 https://www.mnsenaterepublicans.com/wp-content/uploads/2020/10/Review-of-Lawlessness-and-Government-Responses-to-Minnesotas-2020-Riots.pdf
207 https://www.startribune.com/rebuild-of-3rd-precinct-hq-to-cost-10-million-estimate-says/571768442
208 https://www.thecentersquare.com/minnesota/minnesota-national-guard-riot-response-cost-almost-13-million/article_16435bb2-ac05-11ea-a97d-ef8598ee158c.html
209 https://www.nytimes.com/2021/03/12/us/george-floyd-minneapolis-settlement.html#:~:text=The%20City%20of%20Minneapolis%20agreed,officer%20kneeling%20on%20his%20neck.

210 https://nypost.com/2024/08/16/us-news/tim-walz-slammed-for-white-guy-tacos-joke/
211 https://nypost.com/2024/08/14/us-news/walzs-china-ties-under-scrutiny/
212 https://www.nytimes.com/2024/08/11/us/tim-walz-china.html
213 https://www.breitbart.com/2024-election/2024/08/06/kamala-harris-proud-pick-radical-leftist-tim-walz-running-mate/
214 https://www.nytimes.com/2024/08/11/us/tim-walz-china.html
215 Tim Walz taught at China's state-run Macau Polytechnic University until at least 2007 (nypost.com)
216 https://alphanews.org/man-who-says-he-accompanied-walz-on-trip-to-china-calls-vp-candidate-maoist-to-the-core/
217 https://nypost.com/2024/08/13/us-news/rep-jim-banks-probes-tim-walzs-obvious-security-risk-in-dozen-trips-to-china-while-serving-in-national-guard/
218 https://nypost.com/2024/08/13/us-news/rep-jim-banks-probes-tim-walzs-obvious-security-risk-in-dozen-trips-to-china-while-serving-in-national-guard/; https://theinitium.com/article/20240808-international-tim-walz-fatshan-china-us-relation?inviteToken=uxBQZqrmOd
219 https://www.dailymail.co.uk/news/article-13715483/Tim-Walzs-kamala-harris-vp-running-mate-China.html
220 ttps://nypost.com/2024/08/13/us-news/rep-jim-banks-probes-tim-walzs-obvious-security-risk-in-dozen-trips-to-china-while-serving-in-national-guard/; https://www.wsj.com/world/china/tim-walz-is-fascinated-by-chinaand-disturbed-by-its-human-rights-record-ad280ebd
221 https://www.breitbart.com/politics/2024/08/08/exclusive-seamus-bruner-seven-troubling-tim-walz-connections-to-communist-china/
222 https://www.washingtonpost.com/politics/inside-bernie-sanderss-1988-10-day-honeymoon-in-the-soviet-union/2019/05/02/db543e18-6a9c-11e9-a66d-a82d3f3d96d5_story.html
223 https://alphanews.org/man-who-says-he-accompanied-walz-on-trip-to-china-calls-vp-candidate-maoist-to-the-core/
224 https://www.yahoo.com/news/tim-walzs-long-complicated-history-154526036.html
225 https://www.glennbeck.com/st/podcast Best of the Program | Guests: Peter Schweizer & Carol Roth | 8/14/24

226 https://www.dailymail.co.uk/news/article-13715483/Tim-Walzs-kamala-harris-vp-running-mate-China.html
227 https://www.newspapers.com/image/672345904/?-match=1&terms=%28%22Seven%20Students%20Receive%20China%20Scholarships%22
228 https://www.realclearpolitics.com/video/2024/08/25/schweiz-er_chinese_communist_party_has_been_grooming_tim_walz_he_brought_lots_of_copies_of_maos_little_red_book_back_from_china.html
229 https://alphanews.org/man-who-says-he-accompanied-walz-on-trip-to-china-calls-vp-candidate-maoist-to-the-core/
230 https://www.thegatewaypundit.com/2024/08/kamala-har-ris-chooses-vp-deep-ties-communist-china/?utm_source=ak-dart.com&utm_medium=referral
231 https://www.npr.org/2024/08/19/nx-s1-5081407/tim-walz-chi-na-study-abroad
232 https://nypost.com/2024/08/14/us-news/walzs-china-ties-un-der-scrutiny/; https://www.breitbart.com/politics/2024/04/17/exclusive-blood-money-author-peter-schweizer-dismisses-sin-cerity-of-bidens-china-tariff-tough-talk/
233 https://www.glennbeck.com/st/podcast Best of the Program | Guests: Peter Schweizer & Carol Roth | 8/14/24
234 https://www.glennbeck.com/st/podcast Best of the Program | Guests: Peter Schweizer & Carol Roth | 8/14/24
235 https://www.bbc.com/news/world-asia-china-48621202
236 https://www.glennbeck.com/st/podcast Best of the Program | Guests: Peter Schweizer & Carol Roth | 8/14/24
237 https://www.fmprc.gov.cn/web/gjhdq_676201/gj_676203/bmz_679954/1206_680528/1206x2_680548/201901/t20190111_9364607.shtml
238 https://www.breitbart.com/politics/2024/08/08/exclusive-sea-mus-bruner-seven-troubling-tim-walz-connections-to-commu-nist-china/
239 https://nypost.com/2023/04/18/chinese-police-stations-alleged-ly-spyingon-nyc-la-more/
240 https://www.uscc.gov/sites/default/files/annual_reports/2016 Annual Report to Congress.pdf
241 http://qwgzyj.gqb.gov.cn/178/2467.shtml

242 https://www.statesman.com/story/news/politics/politifact/2024/04/30/politifact-are-there-really-chinese-sleeper-cells-operating-in-the-u-s/73475305007/

243 https://www.breitbart.com/asia/2024/08/14/peter-schweizer-democrat-vp-pick-tim-walz-tied-chinese-secret-police-stations-kidnap-ccp-critics/?utm_source=akdart.com&utm_medium=referral

244 https://www.breitbart.com/asia/2024/08/14/peter-schweizer-democrat-vp-pick-tim-walz-tied-chinese-secret-police-stations-kidnap-ccp-critics/?utm_source=akdart.com&utm_medium=referral

245 https://dailycaller.com/2023/06/17/china-intelligence-service-centers-ccp/

246 https://www.breitbart.com/asia/2024/08/14/peter-schweizer-democrat-vp-pick-tim-walz-tied-chinese-secret-police-stations-kidnap-ccp-critics/?utm_source=akdart.com&utm_medium=referral

247 https://globalminnesota.org/event/urban-expedition-2022-china/

248 https://www.iheart.com/content/glenn-beck-blog-is-tim-walz-a-fellow-traveler-with-the-chinese-communist-party/

249 https://tennesseestar.com/politics/tim-walz-has-a-history-of-rubbing-elbows-with-nonprofit-linked-to-chinese-intel-and-influence-agency/dcnf/2024/08/29/

250 https://www.bbc.com/news/articles/cvgewpzyd91o

251 https://www.cnn.com/2024/08/07/media/right-wing-media-tim-walz-harris-attacks-vp-election/index.html

252 https://www.nytimes.com/2024/08/11/us/tim-walz-china.html

253 https://www.washingtonpost.com/opinions/2024/08/08/walz-harris-campaign-china-experience/

254 https://www.npr.org/2024/08/19/nx-s1-5081407/tim-walz-china-study-abroad

255 https://www.yahoo.com/news/tim-walzs-long-complicated-history-154526036.html

256 https://abcnews.go.com/Politics/gops-comer-launches-investigation-walzs-engagement-china/story?id=112896060

257 https://www.breitbart.com/politics/2024/08/08/exclusive-seamus-bruner-seven-troubling-tim-walz-connections-to-communist-china/

258 https://time.com/7008637/tim-walz-china-history-visits-relationship-positions-trade-human-rights/
259 https://www.realclearpolitics.com/video/2024/08/25/schweizer_chinese_communist_party_has_been_grooming_tim_walz_he_brought_lots_of_copies_of_maos_little_red_book_back_from_china.html
260 Engels, *The Origin of the Family, Private Property and the State* (1884)
261 Friedrich Engels, *The Origin of the Family, Private Property and the State* https://www.marxists.org/archive/engels/1884/origin-family/; David McLellan, *Marxism and the Family* https://books.google.com/books/about/Marxism_and_the_Family.html?id=5Ff0oQAACAAJ; Scott Klausen, *The Sexual Revolution in the Soviet Union* https://www.jstor.org/stable/10.2307/2785989; Mary Nolan, *Revolution and Sexuality in the Soviet Union;* https://www.cambridge.org/core/journals/historical-journal/article/revolution-and-sexuality-in-the-soviet-union/
262 https://alphanews.org/man-who-says-he-accompanied-walz-on-trip-to-china-calls-vp-candidate-maoist-to-the-core/
263 Marx and Engels, "The Communist Manifesto," https://www.marxists.org/archive/marx/works/1848/communist-manifesto/
264 Marx and Engels, "The Communist Manifesto," https://www.marxists.org/archive/marx/works/1848/communist-manifesto/
265 Lenin, "What Is to Be Done?" https://www.marxists.org/archive/lenin/works/1901/witbd/
266 Trotsky, "The History of the Russian Revolution," https://www.marxists.org/archive/trotsky/1930/hrr/
267 https://alphanews.org/man-who-says-he-accompanied-walz-on-trip-to-china-calls-vp-candidate-maoist-to-the-core/
268 https://www.youtube.com/watch?v=M6l0tWX7DpM
269 https://en.wikipedia.org/wiki/Four_Olds; https://x.com/Timpanist/status/1819254037629259862
270 https://en.wikipedia.org/wiki/Sweep_Away_All_Cow_Demons_and_Snake_Spirits
271 https://www.marxists.org/archive/lenin/works/1917/staterev/).
272 (Stalin, "Foundations of Leninism," https://www.marxists.org/reference/archive/stalin/works/1924/foundations-leninism/ch02.htm

273 https://freebeacon.com/democrats/speaking-truth-to-vibes-inside-the-mainstream-media-echo-chamber-on-joyful-warrior-kamala-harris/
274 https://www.youtube.com/watch?v=XP7wiRnnBRU
275 Marx, "The Communist Manifesto," https://www.marxists.org/archive/marx/works/1848/communist-manifesto
276 Lenin, "State and Revolution," https://www.marxists.org/archive/lenin/works/1917/staterev/
277 Stalin, "Foundations of Leninism," https://www.marxists.org/reference/archive/stalin/works/1924/foundations-leninism/ch02.htm
278 Khrushchev, "Khrushchev Remembers," https://www.goodreads.com/book/show/1346224.Khrushchev_Remembers
279 https://x.com/Timpanist/status/1819254037629259862
280 https://www.washingtonpost.com/opinions/2024/08/15/kamala-harris-price-gouging-groceries/
281 https://www.washingtonpost.com/business/2024/08/15/kamala-harris-economic-policy-2024/?itid=lk_inline_manual_8
282 https://www.congress.gov/bill/116th-congress/senate-bill/3853/text?s=1&r=85
283 https://www.nytimes.com/2021/03/02/business/gasoline-price-controls.html
284 https://mises.org/library/consequences-price-controls; https://www.cato.org/publications/price-controls-and-market-failures; https://www.reuters.com/breakingviews/big-government-will-drive-next-market-cycle-2023-10-31/
285 Marx, "Das Kapital," https://www.marxists.org/archive/marx/works/1867-c1/
286 Lenin, "The State and Revolution," https://www.marxists.org/archive/lenin/works/1917/staterev/
287 https://freebeacon.com/democrats/speaking-truth-to-vibes-inside-the-mainstream-media-echo-chamber-on-joyful-warrior-kamala-harris/
288 https://2017-2021.state.gov/the-chinese-communist-party-threatening-global-peace-and-security/
289 https://nypost.com/2024/08/13/us-news/rep-jim-banks-probes-tim-walzs-obvious-security-risk-in-dozen-trips-to-china-while-serving-in-national-guard/
290 https://alphanews.org/man-who-says-he-accompanied-walz-on-trip-to-china-calls-vp-candidate-maoist-to-the-core/

291 https://alphanews.org/man-who-says-he-accompanied-walz-on-trip-to-china-calls-vp-candidate-maoist-to-the-core/
292 https://www.glennbeck.com/st/podcast Best of the Program | Guests: Peter Schweizer & Carol Roth | 8/14/24
293 https://x.com/benshapiro/status/1825648939900502330
294 The KARE 11 News at 6 in Minnesota
295 https://x.com/KangHexin/status/1820998923626148218/photo/1
296 https://www.foxnews.com/video/6361358094112
297 https://www.breitbart.com/2024-election/2024/08/06/kamala-harris-proud-pick-radical-leftist-tim-walz-running-mate/
298 Personal interview with Rep. Walter Hudson
299 https://www.startribune.com/unauthorized-immigrants-may-apply-for-minnesota-drivers-licenses-without-proof-of-legal-residency/600310671
300 https://www.foxnews.com/politics/rnc-blasts-walz-admin-non-answer-how-noncitizens-made-minnesota-voter-rolls-no-hypothetical
301 https://www.foxnews.com/video/6361358094112
302 Personal interview with Rep. Walter Hudson

ABOUT THE AUTHORS

JOSH MANNING

Josh Manning serves as The Western Journal's deputy managing editor, holds a master's degree from Harvard University, and has a background in higher education.

ERIN BROWNBACK

Erin Brownback is a messaging strategist specializing in nuanced communications for political, business, and mission-driven clients, and holds a master's degree from Carnegie Mellon University.

www.ingramcontent.com/pod-product-compliance
Ingram Content Group UK Ltd.
Pitfield, Milton Keynes, MK11 3LW, UK
UKHW021701190726
13853UKWH00001B/394